Stewards of the
Mysteries of God

Stewards of the Mysteries of God

Preaching the Old Testament—and the New

PATRICK D. MILLER

CASCADE *Books* · Eugene, Oregon

STEWARDS OF THE MYSTERIES OF GOD
Preaching the Old Testament—and the New

Cascade Books
An Imprint of Wipf and Stock Publishers
199 W. 8th Ave., Suite 3
Eugene, OR 97401

www.wipfandstock.com

ISBN 13: 978-1-62032-551-3

Cataloguing-in-Publication data:

Miller, Patrick D.

Stewards of the mysteries of God : preaching the Old Testament—and the New / Patrick D. Miller ; Foreword by Fleming Rutledge.

xviii + 180 pp. ; 23 cm. Includes bibliographical references and index.

ISBN 13: 978-1-62032-551-3

1. Bible. O.T.—Homiletical use 2. Bible. N.T.—Homiletical use. 3. Bible. O.T.—Sermons. 4. Bible. N.T.—Sermons. 5. Preaching. I. Rutledge, Fleming. II. Title.

BS1191.5 M55 2013

Manufactured in the USA

ACKNOWLEDGMENTS

The author and the publisher gratefully acknowledge the permission of the original publishers of these essays.

"Preaching and Teaching the Old Testament." In *Loving God with our Minds: The Pastor as Theologian: Essays in Honor of Wallace M. Alston,* edited by Michael Welker and Cynthia A. Jarvis, 181–94. Grand Rapids: Eerdmans, 2004.

"Preaching the Old Testament at Easter." *Journal for Preachers* 26/3 (2003) 3–9.

"Preaching Repentance in a Narcissistic Age: Psalm 51." *Journal for Preachers* 21/2 (1998) 3–8.

"Preaching the Ten Commandments." *Journal for Preachers* 25/2 (2002) 3–10.

"Preaching the First Commandment in a Pluralistic Age." *Journal for Preachers* 27/4 (2004) 4–11.

"When Christ Calls." *Princeton Seminary Bulletin* 11 (1990) 143–48.

"What You Need to Know." *Princeton Seminary Bulletin* 14 (1993), 236–39.

"The Prophets' Sons and Daughters." *Princeton Seminary Bulletin* 22 (2001) 279–84.

"Stewards of the Mysteries of God." *Princeton Seminary Bulletin* 25 (2004) 254–58.

"Precious in the Sight of the Lord." *Journal for Preachers* 19/2 (1996) 28–31.

"Heaven." *Presbyterian Outlook* October 10, 2005, 8–9.

"We Are the Lord's." *Princeton Seminary Bulletin* 24 (2003) 190–193.

"The Glory of God and Human Glory." *Princeton Seminary Bulletin* 8 (1987) 66–72.

Once again,
to
Mary Ann

Contents

Contents

Foreword

THIS COLLECTION OF Patrick Miller's essays and sermons is a precious gift to the church in a time of great need. I am privileged to recommend it on two significant counts. It is an enlightened guide for those who would understand and interpret Scripture today, and it offers shining examples of the preaching and study of the Old Testament in particular.

It is a commonplace that today's churchgoers are woefully ignorant of their own Scriptures. We are suffering from a famine of the Word of God, like the one so passionately lamented by the prophet Amos (8:11–12). The causes of this decline are many and various, and there is little profit to be had in enumerating them here; a more positive and hopeful point is that this is a decisive moment in the history of preaching and teaching the Bible. The long reign of "scientific" biblical criticism is over. The so-called historical-critical method was taught in seminaries and theological colleges for the past century; such learning is valuable and indeed inevitable, but it has now given us just about all it has to give. Not everyone in the academic world agrees with that statement, of course, but the turn toward a more literary and theological approach to the whole canon of Scripture has been so decisive that it has become increasingly obvious that textual criticism and historical inquiry per se cannot revive the pulpit. Most preachers know this, at least intuitively, as evidenced by the great increase in storytelling or narrative sermons, designed to "turn to the listener." The problem remains, however, that without total and continual immersion in "the strange new world of the Bible," the preacher will only be able to tell stories from his or her personal human perspective, relating them almost incidentally to the readings for the day—thereby failing to transmit the world-overturning, *kosmos*-re-creating nature of the Voice of God.

Pat Miller is one of those churchmen who, in spite of stellar academic training and preeminent standing among fellow scholars, never lost sight of his identity as one who stands humbly under that living Voice. That's why readers of this volume will find its content so profoundly enriching and upbuilding. This is a resource to turn to for examples of not only how to preach from both Testaments at funerals and at Christmas, but also of how to tell the story of the mighty acts of God as if for the first time. In particular, Miller preaches out of a lifetime's engagement with the Old Testament. These pages are therefore not only filled with *instruction about* the Old Testament, but with the thrilling *news from* the Old Testament.

For make no mistake, the Old Testament in its canonical form is our source for hearing the Voice of the Father of the Lord Jesus Christ. It is not sufficiently understood by Christians today that the Old Testament is the only Bible that Jesus knew, the only Bible that Paul knew, the only Bible that the first apostles knew. As Jesus grew up, he heard the Old Testament Scriptures read every day by his parents and regularly in the synagogue. That was the source of his knowledge of his Father. As Luke 4:21–22 clearly illustrates, it was the Old Testament that Jesus read in order to proclaim who he was and what he came to do. The "it was said of old . . . , but I say unto you" utterances of Jesus in Matthew 5 are not sayings *against* the supposed "God of the Old Testament but are an *illumination of* the Father, now embodied in Jesus himself as the incarnate Word interpreted by the Spirit— a good illustration of the way the Holy Trinity works. (And parenthetically, the Gospel of Matthew, as Pat Miller knows very well, is not just a collection of parables, teachings, and sayings, but is shaped by a lofty Christology.) The challenge of preaching from the Old Testament consists, in part, of hearing the canonical text the way that Jesus himself, and the apostles and evangelists taught by the Spirit, heard it and read it. We must not detach Jesus from what is called in the New Testament, simply, "the scriptures." His entire life was conducted "according to the scriptures," that is, from the perspective and with the power of the God who speaks in the Old Testament.

The challenge for Christian interpretation of the Old Testament is particular since the Holocaust and the emergence of the nation of Israel. The church has suffered from a failure of nerve in this regard. Reactions to the monstrous history of anti-Semitism in the twentieth and twenty-first centuries can be described crudely in two ways, neither of them fully theological. One way is to capitulate entirely, partly if not entirely out of guilt, by relinquishing the church's confession of the Old Testament as Christian Scripture. Another way is incipiently anti-Judaic, epitomized in the pervasive misapprehension about the wrathful God of the Old Testament over against the merciful God of the New Testament. This widespread misunderstanding is so deeply lodged in the minds of many church members that only a very concerted, intentional remedial program of extending over a period of years can displace it. The primary way to do this is to preach the gospel from the Old Testament in an ongoing, comprehensive fashion, and Pat Miller has shown us how in this most valuable collection.

Robert Jenson has famously written, "God . . . raised Jesus from the dead, having before raised Israel from Egypt."[1] This dictum is a corrective to the widespread tendency among Christians toward a "Jesus *kerygma*" detached from the story of God's dealings with the Hebrew people. Indeed, it is remarkable that whereas, only a few decades ago, many liberal mainline preachers avoided frequent use of the name of Jesus in sermons because they feared being thought unsophisticated or "evangelical," the opposite problem is now the case. Stories from the life and ministry of Jesus can be and often are told without any reference to God. The common practice in churches that use a lectionary of preaching mostly from the Synoptic Gospels has greatly exacerbated this unfortunate tendency. It is extraordinary that this has occurred concurrently with the concern of the mainline churches to avoid offense to Jews. In fact, it is precisely a heavy dose of Old Testament teaching that provides the antidote to a truncated understanding of biblical faith. We must not separate Jesus from the God who is praised in the Psalms, who called the prophets, who intervened in such a shockingly particularly way in human history.

We have been speaking of preaching, but it is not only preachers who will find treasures throughout these pages. Laypeople who yearn to hear life-giving sermons and biblical teaching will find rich nourishment in Miller's book as well, and may indeed discover how to encourage their own clergy. Lowered expectations in many congregations have led to resignation about uninspired preaching; when one has read or heard sermons from the Old Testament at the level of those in this volume, it will be difficult to be satisfied with anything less. The seminaries and theological colleges should take note as well, for there is no greater need in the church today than to reconnect the Testaments so that the whole sweep of the sacred story can be heard afresh. There is joy and wonder to be found in the discovery that the two Testaments illumine one another in equal measure. For as the apostle Paul wrote in one of his most ardent passages,

> For I delivered to you as of first importance what I also received, that Christ died for our sins *in accordance with the scriptures*, that he was buried, that he was raised on the third day *in accordance with the scriptures.* (1 Cor 15:3–4)

1. Jenson, *Systematic Theology*, 1:63. Miller has himself quoted this in a previous essay.

Professor Miller has wonderfully shown us in these pages, not only how to preach Jesus Christ and the Triune God in accordance with the Old Testament Scriptures, but how to live in the light of the promises of the Holy One of Israel.

Fleming Rutledge
author of *And The Lord Spoke to Abraham*
Rye Brook, New York

Michaelmas 2012

Preface

THE ESSAYS AND SERMONS in this book grew out of my years as a seminary teacher. While preaching is not a regular part of that vocation, it is often a responsibility of the teacher, either within the parameters of the teaching vocation and its locale or in different churches and with regard to different aspects of the preaching and teaching ministry. While my life as a minister began with about three years as pastor of a small Presbyterian church in South Carolina, none of the sermons come from that time. It was very much a time of learning, of finding out what it is like to enter the pulpit every seven days and preach a sermon to an expectant congregation that is there to hear the Word preached and learn how it touches and molds their lives. Nothing was more formative and important for my teaching vocation than that experience. But the time of learning was clearly that, so the sermons published here belong to later years of more experience and maturity. And while they do not grow out of a pastorate, they are often set in some clear context that shapes the sermon and is reflected in it, whether that be a July 4th Sunday, Advent and Christmas, a pastor's ordination, a funeral service, seminary graduation, or an occasion of Holy Communion.

The title is an accurate reflection of the intentionality of this collection. The essays focus particularly on preaching the Old Testament. The first two of these are more reflective and speak more generally and broadly about what belongs to the preaching of the Old Testament. The ones that follow take up particular Old Testament texts or groups of texts seeking to uncover and talk about aspects and dimensions that belong to their preaching. In this combination of broader reflection on the place of the Old Testament in the church's preaching and explicit suggestions of how Old Testament texts may be interpreted and preached, I have tried to provide a foundation of understanding the Old Testament as the preachable Word, guidelines for taking up texts, and specific examples of texts being interpreted.

Inevitably this involves some reflection on the way in which the Old Testament relates to the New Testament. As the title of this collection indicates, I do not separate one Testament from the other. Preaching the Old Testament always involves awareness of the whole of Scripture, as does any preaching from the New. While I often find myself preaching from Old Testament texts (sometimes, I think, simply because I am familiar with them and spend time with them), just as often the focus of a sermon will be a New Testament text; or a New Testament text or story inevitably and necessarily makes its way into the sermon (see, for example, "The Glory of God and Human Glory"). Similarly, Old Testament texts make their way into sermons arising out of a New Testament passage (see "We Are the Lord's"). Often the sermon is based on texts from both Testaments. As I hope the sermons and essays make clear, there is no one way in which the Testaments are preached and related to each other. They and their content are always there as a part of the preaching, however their interrelationship is indicated—or not—in the preached sermon. One of the important aspects of the church's titles for these Scriptures—Old Testament and New Testament—is their holding the two bodies of texts in relation to each other and raising the question of how they interact with each other. A sermon on an Old Testament text may reach its climax as it moves into the New Testament or engages a New Testament text. But it also may proclaim the gospel without even moving to a New Testament text. Good preaching of the Bible constantly seeks for the resonances between the Testaments. And that can happen in various ways.

Readers of the sermons in this book will become aware of two things—at least. One is the prevalence of storytelling and particularly the personal stories. We talk much about illustrations and their significance for preaching. Perhaps that category is a broad enough one to cover any connection the preacher makes between the text and the contemporary context, or any effort to use something outside of Scripture to illumine the text and its interpretation. I would suggest, however, that it is particularly the human stories we live and remember that especially help us connect with the text and its message.

Another characteristic of the sermons collected here is that they not infrequently echo each other and reiterate some basic themes. That is especially noticeable, for example, in the three sermons preached at funeral services, but it is evident elsewhere as well. While one may call that repetition, and sometimes it is, the reiteration serves also to lift up some of the things that matter most and give them a kind of emphasis.

Except for the funeral sermons, I have not tried to identify the original contexts for the sermons, some of which have been preached more than once. At times, readers will be able to identify a general context by virtue of the subject matter or the way the congregation is addressed. Inevitably, much of that context is the theological seminary where the practice of ministry is what unites all who serve and work there. This means, of course, that much of the preaching is about the ministry. I hope even those sermons may demonstrate appropriate and helpful ways of preaching the Old Testament—and the New—in other settings and contexts.

Essays

ONE

The Old Testament in the Pulpit[1]

THE OLD TESTAMENT IN THE CHRISTIAN CANON

I WANT TO BEGIN our time together by an invitation to you to study and preach and teach the Old Testament in the years ahead in your ministry. It is a genuine invitation in that studying and preaching the Old Testament is not an automatic happening in the Christian pulpit. It is a serious invitation also because it is something I believe you will enjoy doing. The study of the Old Testament may change your life. At least it did mine. Not simply in that it gave me something to do for which someone paid me a decent salary. That is true, and I am grateful. But I am not talking about stumbling onto a way to earn a living. I am talking about stumbling into a world whose central character has taken hold of my life and is taking hold of your life. And the one place where you can make sense of that is in these Scriptures.

I want, then, to lift up *four* things about the Old Testament that are presuppositions for its serious interpretation and preaching.

1. The first is that learning to be a good and faithful interpreter of Scripture means learning to live in the *tension* between receiving and studying the Bible as *an ancient record* of the experience and testimony of an ancient people, Israel, and receiving it as *the powerful word of God* to the present people of God here and now. These Scriptures come from a period literally thousands of years ago, in a foreign language that is not the easiest thing to master. They are often offensive

---

1. This essay originated in comments to introductory seminary courses in Old Testament and exegesis.

as they speak in explicit detail about sex, murder, rape, abused wives, and other equally unpleasant and disturbing matters. Things happen within the Old Testament that may make little sense in our context. We cannot ignore the distance of the text from us or the demands that distance places upon us to work to try to understand these words from long ago.

With all of that, however, the text is also the word of God that transcends every time and place. It has the capacity to connect with us and who and what we are, to speak from a distant and alien time a word that challenges and comforts us, that speaks truth to power and goodness to evil. Our interest in these books is not finally antiquarian; it is so that we can learn better how to praise God and to live our lives.

2. A second thing I want to say is a word about *what the Old Testament offers us*. It is the record of Israel's struggle to be the people of God. It deals with family history and family stories, with tribal history, monarchical regimes, and court intrigue, with minority groups and oppressed peoples. The strangeness and distance of these books cannot conceal the way they deal with and in this world in which we live, where nations are at war, where tribalism and ethnic cleansing lead to slaughter and destruction of neighbors, where human beings experience the deepest pain and cry out for help not knowing whether their cry will ever be heard, where the life and death of families and nations are the context in which the providence of God is wrought out, where goodness and blessing are God's intention for all of life. The Old Testament is rooted deeply in this world, in the terrors and possibilities of human life under God, in the conflicts of peoples and nations. There may be a lot of angels and divine beings around, but there is an *earthiness* to the Old Testament that always seems to resonate with the earthiness of this dust and clay that compose our beings. If the Old Testament dares to say, as it does over and over again, that God is with us and God will help us, it does so clearly aware of all there is in human life that calls that into question. Indeed all the questions that *you* could ever think to ask *about* God or *to* God, in doubt or in pain, have already come from the lips of ancient Israel.

3. The third thing I would have you keep in mind is that *the Old Testament belongs with the New and the New Testament belongs with the Old*. In its own right the authoritative word of the Lord, the Old Testament

is also the deep and rich quarry out of which the New Testament was hewn. The Old Testament books are the Scriptures of Jesus Christ and the best clue we have to who and what he was and what he was about. When the early church sought to understand this one who had come into their midst, claiming them for his discipleship and service in the kingdom of God, they turned to the Scriptures of the Torah, the Prophets, and the Writings, that is, to the Old Testament. *There is nothing new that the New Testament tells us about God and God's ways with us and for us. All is revealed in the Old Testament.* What the New Testament does is identify the one in whom God is at work to fulfill those purposes set from the beginning.

As he sat in prison awaiting the possibility of execution, the German pastor and theologian Dietrich Bonhoeffer warned against getting to the New Testament too soon without hearing that full word of the Old Testament. It is that word we want to hear. When we do, it will resonate and point beyond itself to our Lord and to our life. When we understand it well, then we can understand that other Testament better.

So learn to live in that tension between, on the one hand, not going to the New Testament too quickly so that you really do hear the Word of God in the Old Testament, for it is there as clearly as in the New; and, on the other hand, hearing the Old Testament always as a word that has to do with the one who is our Lord. There is never any need to *search* for Christ in the text of the Old Testament. But you will often *encounter* him there or know that what you read and hear is the one word of the one God whom we have come to know in Jesus Christ.

4. Finally, the Old Testament as part of the canon of Scripture *exercises a claim upon us* and we want to be open to that. In a sense, I am now talking about its authority, though I am less interested in the grounds of that authority—which I think are fairly clear—than in its effects. The Old Testament takes its place as Scripture for us; that is, the Word of God becomes the word for us when a number of things happen:

- when it calls us into a community that has transcendent dimensions and believes that there is more to this world than our human existence;

- when it calls us into a community that is defined from outside the corruption of history and the failings of human beings, even as it is made up of such folks, just like ourselves;

- when it creates visions and sings songs of impossibilities not yet imagined in this world: visions of a kingdom of righteousness and peace, of a new humanity, of the poor become rich and the lowly lifted up and the barren fertile, of swords into plowshares and guns into tractors;

- when it speaks in a way that transforms lives from being self-centered to being God centered.

I know nothing more demanding, exhilarating, or needed in this world than the effort to hear and proclaim those things from Scripture. I do not think you will find much in your ministry more meaningful or fulfilling than that.

ON THE MOVEMENT FROM EXEGESIS TO PREACHING

1. The outcome of your interpretive work is always in mind from the beginning. You do not turn to the text and say, I will find out what this means and then think about preaching from it. You are from the start listening for and looking for the ways the text opens up to communicate a word from the Lord to your congregation. This is why for me, one of the most profitable aspects of the interpretive process is a direct reading of the text in English but with an open interpretive agenda; that is, looking for what I can see about the limits of the text: its structure and shape, what its subject matter is and what is said about it, repetitions that may identify emphases, and the like. I begin making notes about what I discern, starting from the beginning to articulate and imagine what one might say. James L. Mays has properly described exegesis as disciplined meditation on the text.

2. The further work of exegesis allows one to test those first forays and to go deeper into the text, but it is still part of an ongoing process that ends up in the preached text. I do not know where the line between exegesis and preaching is drawn, but let me suggest a possible way of keeping the movement going. That is to let your exegetical work culminate in some effort to state what you see as the intention of the

text, its basic claim(s), what it is after, what matters about it. There is no single term that is all-sufficient to describe this way of pulling one's work together. It is not a summary of your work or of the text. It is beginning to say "This is what I think this text is about. This is what it is after and seeks to communicate."

3. As you keep trying to say what that claim or intention is, as you keep articulating and spelling it out, you will find yourself more and more moving toward the preaching of the text. It is not so much that one says, Okay, now how do I preach this text? You have already been wrestling with and working on that all along the way. And you keep on talking about the text, and before you know it, you are into the way the text communicates the word of the Lord to the contemporary community of faith. Now you are going to have to craft the sermon still, of course. But it will be crafted around what you have come to understand *and articulate* about what matters about the text, the *so what?* of the text. But you have had that question in your mind all the time.

4. At the same time, I want to recognize that the focus of a sermon may be on a particular element in the text, something that your interpretive work has identified as an important aspect of its communication, a particular verse that has something to say. It may be in some sense the key verse of the text, or it may be a separate point or matter within the whole.

5. The communication of the text will be most helpful to those to whom you are preaching or teaching if two things happen, and they stand in some tension with one another:

    a. Do not let go of the text, long or short. Respect it; attend to it; let the congregation be fed by it. Communicate it, illustrate, explain. Do not let your self get in the way of it or lose it. You will be surprised how much your people really do want to be fed by the word of Scripture.

    b. At the same time, the preaching will be strongest if it is *theological* and not simply an exposition of the text. Hold those things together. As you have grasped what the text is about, develop its theological character and implications as best you can. The preaching is deeply rooted in the text, but it is also theological and pastoral.

6. Do not let yourself get caught in the assumption that you have to end up by taking the text and the sermon into the New Testament. If the text pulls you that way for certain reasons, then by all means go with it. But remember that your congregation is a community of Christians who have the New Testament, who are disciples of Jesus Christ, and so who assume that the text and its preaching belong in that context. Do not get hooked on a single way of relating the Old Testament text to the New, especially on the easy and often misleading and unhelpful schema of promise and fulfillment. That really may fit for Advent, say, but often does not and is not helpful. Look rather for the resonances and the continuities between the Old Testament text and the New Testament. Presume the wholeness and unity of the canon and let that come to light. What you want to try to avoid is a kind of mechanical move to the New Testament that seems either forced or predictable, as if the sermon is not complete unless somehow we refer to Jesus or the New Testament. Let the connections arise out of the text before you.

TWO

Preaching and Teaching
the Old Testament

THE LIFE OF THE church centers on the word. When Karl Barth began
his *Church Dogmatics* with an articulation of the threefold form of the
word of God (proclamation, Scripture, and revelation), he rightly identified
the beginning point of theology and ethics, of faith and practice.[1] In what
it does and what it thinks, the Christian community and specifically its
manifestation in the form of the congregation, is inseparable from the word
in its threefold form. Of course, this may not be the case in practice. But the
principle is so clear that failure so to live and think, that is, failure to place
at the center of the church's life the word in its three forms, is to skew and
distort the very character of the community of faith as the church. For this
reason, the church's ministry is by definition a ministry of the word. It is a
ministry that constantly points to Christ, places all of life and thought in
the light of Scripture, and regularly engages in proclamation of the word.[2]

Indeed one might argue on very practical grounds that the interpretation of the word as a theological enterprise is the peculiar task of ministry
in the sense that it is the one activity of the church's life for which the pastor
is truly the resident expert. The capacity to bring the light of Scripture and
theology to whatever is happening is the one thing that the pastor provides that is not available elsewhere in the life of the congregation, where
there are not other and better experts (for example, in financial matters,

---

1. Barth, *Church Dogmatics*, I/1.

2. I realize that in the Reformed tradition we speak of the ministry of the word and
sacraments, but in this instance I am subsuming the sacraments within the word, recog-
nizing that the sacraments are a materialization of faith and practice as given to us in the
word and thus not themselves separate from the word.

administration, counseling, education, and the like) often available and a part of the congregation. If the pastor of the congregation is no longer necessarily the most highly educated person and the most knowledgeable in all aspects of the church's life, she or he is still the one who brings understanding of the faith and interpretation of the word to bear on the life of the congregation. The ministry of the word is the primary task of the pastor of the congregation.

This fundamental assumption has obvious implications for theological education. If Scripture is going to shape life and thought for the church *and especially for the ministry,* then a sense of that ought to pervade the theological curriculum. As the center of the curriculum, the Bible is not the focus of the whole of the curriculum. But it is the pivot around which all other matters revolve, and it is the center that helps define what is more marginal and peripheral. That some aspects of theological education are more peripheral, of course, does not make them unimportant.

More Bible courses, per se, are not what is really at stake, although one might well argue that in many seminaries outside evangelical circles, the actual teaching of Scripture has been squeezed to a very minimum. But the minister is a theologian, and once that is seen as the primary characterization of her or his role, then it is clear that the Bible is the source and ground for many dimensions of the work of ministry, and the carefully prepared minister needs to be able to draw upon that source in a variety of ways that require various kinds of knowledge and skill acquisition. The issue is not Bible versus theology but whether or not the theologian-minister does his or her theology in a sophisticated conversation with Scripture, a conversation that begins to be learned in seminary only as teachers of Scripture assume a theological responsibility for the texts they interpret and the content they teach, and as theologians develop an understanding of doctrine and its history that is rooted in Scripture.[3] Gerhard Ebeling has argued that

3. I have used the word *sophisticated* intentionally even though some may see that as a weasel word or a cover for license in the handling of Scripture. It is instead a replacement for the customary adjective *critical.* I assume the critical aspect of one's sophisticated reading of Scripture, but that is not all that is involved. The best term might be *mature.* What is envisioned is the kind of understanding of Scripture and theology that comes from deep study of both, practice in the interpretation of Scripture, familiarity with hermeneutical issues and principles, and a theological framework that informs the understanding of texts and is open to revision in the light of their interpretation. All of that takes time, learning, and practice. It also involves creativity, intuition, and imagination. Some persons are better at such sophisticated interpretation than others, but all may continue to develop in that direction.

the history of the church is essentially the history of the interpretation of Scripture.[4] Many historians of the church and of doctrine may find that definition too limiting, but there is a large element of truth to it, and it at least suggests that the teaching of history is not something apart from the preparation of ministers for thinking about how the Bible shapes life and thought—then and now. There is little creedal activity that has not been a wrestling with Scripture, and the most heated controversies of the last half century in the North American church—for example, segregation and racism in American life, the morality of war and the place of the conscience, the nature and value of human life, appropriate understanding and worship of God, and the church's attitude toward same-sex relations—have been vigorous debates about what Scripture teaches and how we are to be directed by Scripture.

The issue, then, is the acknowledgment by those who teach in theological education that whatever we do, whether it is interpretation of texts—where the Bible is front and center—or practice in homiletics, or the teaching of doctrine, our subject matter in some ways is constantly engaged with the Bible. Critical to such an acknowledgment (by which I do not mean paying lip service to the importance of Scripture, but rather letting that awareness be an influential and determinative criterion) is the recognition that the Bible is not a specialized area to be left in the hands of Scripture scholars but is the subject matter of all the fields. As the church has always had to live in the tension between affirming the clarity of Scripture and knowing its difficult and dark places, and in the tension between receiving Scripture as an ancient, foreign, literary document and as the word of God, so it must also live in the tension between (on the one hand) insisting that some of its teachers and doctors devote themselves to a deep and technical knowledge and competence in the Scriptures, and (on the other hand) holding all other teachers to a responsibility for thinking and teaching in relation to the Word even as they are committed to the development of technical knowledge and skill in other areas of the theological enterprise. This is not an easy task, and the tendency is always to compartmentalize Scripture; that is, for the biblical scholars to claim it, either consciously or unconsciously, as their own domain; and for the theologians, historians, and practical theologians to assign it to the biblical scholars in order to get on with their own large tasks. The problem is that those large tasks have too much to do with the Bible for such segmentation to work. The

4. Ebeling, *Kirchengeschichte*.

pastor, whose education is the responsibility of the seminary, is not allowed to separate in this fashion. There is no point where she or he does not have to bring the Bible into conversation with all sorts of things in this world, and nowhere that the pastor can expect to escape some accountability to biblical revelation. The seminary is in danger of an artificial and thus countereducational model in its handling of Scripture. At best it is artificial, and at worst it is nonprofessional in that it does not prepare its students for the practice of the profession as it is to be carried out.[5]

One piece of this picture, however, is more fuzzy in conceptuality and less evident in practice. That piece is the Old Testament. We have assumed the inclusion of the Old Testament as a part of the Word that informs faith and life, and in the Reformed tradition have done so more vigorously than may be the case in other branches of the Christian church. But in both theory and practice that inclusion is often fragmentary, subordinate, and peripheral. Or we may be unclear about what role the Old Testament is to play and most especially how we are to regard it in relation to the New Testament and the church's preaching. Some of the problems appear to be endemic to Christian theology, which seems always to be clearer about the function of the New Testament than the Old. By necessity, the church has to keep rethinking how the Old Testament is a part of the word and thus at the center of the church's faith and its ministry.

THE OLD TESTAMENT AS SCRIPTURE

It is as the church reads and interprets the Bible *as a whole* that the Old Testament comes into its place as the word of God. This is a risky business. In our time, we have become highly conscious of the multiple voices of

---

5. One of my most vivid and enduring pedagogical memories is of an extended conversation with a class of students at the conclusion of a course on God in the Old Testament. The first time I had taught the course, I had set it up on a history of religion model. That did not work very well. The second time, partly out of my own awareness and partly out of the natural direction that the students wished to move, the course was more theological in character. At the end, I indicated to the class my strong sense that when I taught the course again, I would need to get a theologian colleague to join me and teach the course as a team. With one voice the class resisted and protested that decision on my part, one that had grown out of my own sense of ineptness in dealing with many of the theological questions and issues that arose in looking at what the Bible says about God. They felt strongly that one of the most important features of the course was precisely my being forced to deal, however ineptly, with all the issues and not only the more strictly biblical ones—exactly as they would have to do in their own ministry.

Scripture and careful about not silencing, distorting, or marginalizing any of these voices. The sense of the whole is there, but it is a whole of many and varied parts, sufficiently different in genre, time, perspective, and the like to dampen serious efforts to think of Scripture primarily as a whole. In the necessary interpretive movement within the hermeneutical circle, we tend to exaggerate the parts and minimize the whole so that the circle is not really maintained. We are afraid that our sense of the whole will distort the parts, so we are careful about articulating the individual voices but resistant to asking how they play their part in and are to be understood in light of the whole. But it is also possible that one may so lack a sufficient sense of the whole that the elements that make it up cannot properly be comprehended *as Scripture*. Interpretation in the light of the rule of faith and the rule of love, even if that is done fairly subconsciously and not overtly, is in order to maintain some sense of the whole and of the character of the Bible as Scripture, the rule of faith and practice.

The danger is already there within the respective Testaments. That is, we are inclined to discern a panoply of theologies within each Testament—the theology of Paul, Johannine theology, and the like. Indeed, Scripture itself encourages us so to view it. After all, the church found four Gospels in its Scripture, and there are clearly significant differences discerned and tensions experienced in their presentations of Jesus Christ. But those four Gospels are a way of saying that the church needs all of this to comprehend who Jesus Christ is and what God was and is doing in him. The neglect of any one of them will skew the Christology of the church even if a harmonization of them is not an easy task and indeed may be impossible.

There is a much larger disjunction, however, between the two parts of the canon, whose formation and character are quite distinct from one another but whose theological wholeness is fundamental to the revelation of God's nature and activity. Because the Old Testament is there, the community of faith knows that God's work in and through Israel is central to what God is doing in the world. Because the New Testament is there, the centrality of Jesus Christ in that divine work in the world is made clear. The church finds the revelation of God's work incomplete without the New Testament. It finds the revelation of God in Jesus Christ both unintelligible and unauthorized without the Old Testament. The interrelation between the two Testaments and the work of God to which they bear testimony may and should be described in different ways, but the centrality of each must be maintained, despite the apparent logical contradiction implied in such a claim.

As the church lives and breathes out of the Scriptures of the Old and New Testaments, it encounters and effects both a *centrifugal* force that tends to push them ever away from one another and a *centripetal* force that tends to draw these Scriptures ever more closely together. The practice of the church is often toward the centrifugal force rather than the centripetal. One reflection of the power of that force is the easy intrusion into theological education and even the practice of ministry of alternative terms for the Old Testament, such as *Hebrew Scriptures*, the *Scriptures of Israel*, *Tanakh*, or the like. The abandonment of the term *Old Testament* has many implications, a few good but others less desirable. The rubrics *Old Testament* and *New Testament* are not to be viewed simply as vestiges of an unenlightened and supersessionist history.[6] They are pointers to the wholeness and indivisibility of Scripture and to a relationship not adequately characterized by alternatives—at least so far—and indeed is significantly diminished—sometimes quite intentionally—by their use. The use of the terms *Hebrew Bible*, *Hebrew Scriptures*, or equivalents may have some practical uses but such substitutes should not become the defining terms in a theological context.[7] To move in that direction is to place the *language* of the Old Testament as definitive when there is no theological or historical reason for doing so;[8]

6. These standard terms may serve a supersessionist reading of the New Testament and God's work in Jesus Christ, which is one of the reasons some would substitute other terms. But that reading is not intrinsic, nor has there been sufficient attention to the deficiencies in the alternatives. Among the most helpful treatments of the larger theological issues underlying this terminological debate is Soulen's *The God of Israel and Christian Theology*. Though he uses the term *Hebrew Scriptures*, he is less concerned with terminology and more with supersessionism as a problem for theology and with the possibility of a theological reading of Scripture that is attentive to the wholeness of Scripture as our best clue to what God is doing in the world but is not supersessionist.

7. Here it is important to distinguish between the very different teaching contexts of university and theological school. In the university, there may very well be good reasons for the use of the valid terms *Hebrew Bible*, *Tanakh*, and the like, though it should not be assumed that any descriptive phrase is somehow neutral and does not make a decision in one direction or another about how this literature is to be viewed, even if the function of a particular term is to make the theological-faith character of the literature more vague. (On this matter, see now the helpful discussion by Seitz, "Old Testament or Hebrew Bible?" The adoption of an alternative to *Old Testament* in the broader academy has been drawn into theological education much too easily and unreflectively.

8. It is perhaps a minor quibble to note that the term is also inaccurate in that some of the Old Testament was originally written in Aramaic. An alternative term that avoids the focus on language is *Israel's Scriptures*. While such a designation is certainly true, it is only half true. Those Scriptures are also the church's scriptures, and so the designation serves once again implicitly to separate the two parts of the Christian Bible from one another and relegate the Old Testament to a secondary position in the church's life.

it focuses on the separation of the Christian Scriptures rather than their unity; and it suggests a wholeness within the Old Testament apart from the other Testament, a position that cannot be maintained in the church, and probably not within Judaism either.[9] Furthermore, it leaves *the New Testament* as an essentially meaningless term, as is recognized by some who have shifted to *Greek Scriptures*, or something similar. The church, in its proclamation and in its preparation for ministry, needs to resist the temptation to solve its supersessionist theological tendencies and problems by the use of nontheological language for speaking about the theological foundation of the church's faith, the Bible.

Even where the church and its teachers hold to a clear conviction about the wholeness of Scripture, in various ways we let them drift apart. One of the more obvious ways is the academic curricular division into Old Testament and New Testament and the corollary division of faculty responsibilities into one or the other Testament. There are good practical reasons for this—division of duties, different languages; but one should not ignore the outcome and the difficulty this division places upon the teachers of Bible—and even more the students—in trying to resist the centrifugal force.

Because the primary subject matter of the Scriptures is the God who is at work in the story they recount and in the world in which we live, the wholeness and coherence of Scripture supersedes its partition. That coherence is real but not self-evident. It may be manifest in various modes. I have already referred to the rule of faith and the rule of love, which are theological and ethical frameworks for perceiving what the Scriptures are about in their entirety.[10] Interpreters have been able also to discern a canon within the canon or a center that holds the whole together in the face of

9. Here I am assuming that the Scriptures that arose out of God's story with Israel are always read in relation to some other body of authoritative or normative literature. For Christians, it is the New Testament; for Jews it is the Talmud. The relation of these other bodies of literature to the biblical literature may vary, but in neither instance can one properly comprehend and define the faith that they nurture without attention to their relation to the other literary corpus that also serves to define the community of faith. This does not mean that the shared biblical literature—Old Testament/Hebrew Bible—cannot be genuinely shared, a point that Walter Brueggemann has demonstrated forcefully and explicitly in his *Theology of the Old Testament*, which insists on much common ground between Jewish and Christian reading of the Old Testament but also easily develops ad hoc relationships between the content of the Old Testament and that of the New.

10. See *The Presbyterian Understanding and Use of Holy Scripture*, a position paper adopted by the 123rd General Assembly (1983) of the former Presbyterian Church in the United States.

the manifold voices. While the danger of reductionism is always evident in such moves, they are necessary. Further, the Scriptures contain a story that has the Lord God at its center as the chief actor. That story, whose foundations are in the Old Testament, is the framework for the whole and provides a structure that gives coherence even though not everything can be located at some specific moment in the story. All that is there belongs to the story and is not to be understood, interpreted, or proclaimed apart from it.

THE OLD TESTAMENT AND CHRIST

The sense of the wholeness, the coherence of Scripture, the manifestation of a centripetal force that holds the Testaments together as a single Scripture, leads one into the effort to understand the relation of the Old Testament to Jesus Christ and vice versa.[11] Efforts to uncover modes of coherence that give full place to the Old Testament nevertheless must tend to the meaning of Jesus Christ in relation to the whole of Scripture and not just the New Testament.

In addition to the structuring coherence provided by the story, the wholeness of Scripture as Scripture may be articulated in several ways that are deeply rooted in the Old Testament:

From beginning to end the *subject matter* of the Bible is *the Lord*, whose name is revealed in the Old Testament and restated in relation to Jesus of Nazareth in the New. The revelation of the name is in the context of the revelation of the words and deeds of the God who created the universe, called Abraham and blessed him and his posterity, and redeemed Israel from its harsh slavery in Egypt. The rest of the story is a further unpacking of that revelation and the meaning of the name. One comes to know who it is that rules this world and has called us into blessing and service, into

---

11. What I am talking about here commonly comes under the rubric "the unity of Scripture." I have no major objection to that term and use it myself. In this context, however, I am appropriating other terms that may, partly in their multiplicity and variety, avoid the dangers of over simplicity and reductionism that sometimes seem to be carried by the term "unity." The notion of coherence allows for significant complexity and assumes differentiation and variety. In this context, I am not making the case for the complexity because, as indicated above, that case is all too prominent and does not need to be made. It is the question of the coherence of the evident complexity that needs attention. For further discussion of this way of thinking about the whole and its parts, see Schweiker and Welker, "A New Paradigm"; and Miller, "A Theocentric Theologian of Hope."

grace and obedience, only as one begins to read the Old Testament. That one, whose name is revealed in the Tetragrammaton *YHWH*, has come to be called "the Lord." The use of the Greek term *kurios* as a surrogate for the divine name in the Old Testament and as address and title for Jesus Christ in the New Testament—a tradition that has carried over into the translations and so has come to be the practice of the church throughout its life—binds the Testaments inextricably together as it identifies the subject of one Testament with that of the other. The church knows this term—and bows before its reality—only as the name of the God of Israel and the Lord of the church.[12]

To the extent that the *name of God* is revelatory, the connections between the name of the God of Israel and Jesus Christ are even stronger than in the shared title *Lord*. The much-discussed and at least ambiguous form of the divine name of God as it is revealed in Exodus 3 gets its primary meaning *contextually*, that is, from the Lord's word to Moses on the occasion of commissioning him to go into Pharaoh. The term *'ehyeh*, which is the word in the divine-name formula *'ehyeh 'asher 'ehyeh* ("I will be what I will be" or "I am who I am"), occurs twice in the Lord's reassurance to Moses: "I will be with you" (Exod 3:12 and 4:12).[13] The story in its full form, therefore, identifies the companioning and protecting presence of God with those who serve and worship the Lord as definitive of who this God is. That claim, of course, is carried over into the name *Immanuel* ("God is with us"), which becomes one of the names of the child born to Mary (Matt 1:23), thus establishing an explicit continuity between the Lord of Israel and the one for whom Israel had hoped, the one who embodies God's companioning presence with the people. The story itself is structured around this revelation of the character of the God of Scripture, first revealed in the Old Testament and confirmed in the Christ of the New Testament, for the last word we hear about this God is the vision of the new heaven and the new earth and the new Jerusalem and the voice from the throne declaring, "Behold, the dwelling of God is with human beings . . . God will be with them" (Rev 21:3). The continuity of name and identity carries forward also

---

12. Technically, the term *Lord* is an epithet and not a proper name, but its substitution for the proper name of God in the Old Testament puts it in a somewhat different category from other epithets, as indicated by the fact that many translations distinguish the use of the term *lord* as a surrogate for the divine name from its use as a common name by setting the former in capital letters.

13. This is most obvious in the parallel expressions in Exod 3:14–15: "*'ehyeh* has sent me to you, // *yhwh* . . . has sent me to you."

in the continuity between the context in which the name of God is revealed, (that is, the Lord's hearing of the cries of the Israelites and coming to deliver them) and the other name of the child of Mary, which is "Jesus," that is, "He will save his people" (Matt 1:21). That the salvation brought by the child is a salvation "from their sins" is an expectation that has arisen explicitly out of the Old Testament (Isa 52:13—53:12).[14]

What this means is that the church hears afresh in the New Testament what it already knows from the Old Testament about God and God's ways with us. For Jesus is no other than who and what God has always been.[15] The theological way of apprehending this is the *doctrine of the Trinity*. The Trinity is a way of speaking theologically about the richness, wholeness, and coherence of *Scripture* as it identifies these very characteristics within the reality of *God* but not as incidental or developing dimensions or as aspects or persons of the Godhead to be identified with one Testament or the other.[16] It is worthy of note that the representation of the three biblical men or angels who appeared to Abraham at the oak of Mamre for many centuries was "the only iconography of the Holy Trinity; it is still preserved in the Orthodox Church as that which accords best with its teaching." The long tradition of the church has found its most durable representation of the Trinity in the depiction of an Old Testament scene.[17]

14. For a more extended presentation of this continuity between the names of God and the names of Jesus, see Miller, *They Cried to the Lord*, 173–77.

15. The point could be elaborated over and over by placing various texts and contexts from both Testaments in conversation with each other, which is what the church has always done. It is important, however, that while notions of promise/prophecy and fulfillment will come to play in such a conversation, that mode of hearing the two Testaments together does not exhaust the way conversation is to be played out. The church has not been helped by confining much of its interpretation of the coherence of Scripture to oppositional motifs (e.g., law and gospel). In this respect, Soulen's book (referred to in n. 6) is quite helpful with its focus on blessing and consummation as ways of discerning the wholeness of Scripture in relation to the whole of the story.

16. "The Old Testament fills our understanding about the nature and character of the first person of the Trinity. It is only on this basis that the church can accept the claim that Jesus is one with God. Within the biblical story, there is an identity between the words and deeds of the Lord of Israel and the Lord of the church that presses upon those who live by that story that they are truly one. It is therefore unlikely that the church can hold its scriptures together without a conviction that in the doctrine of the Trinity, we comprehend something of the fullness of God" (Miller, "A Strange Kind of Monotheism," 296). Cf. Jenson, "The Bible and the Trinity," 329–39.

17. Ouspensky and Lossky, *The Meaning of Icons*, 201.

The *kingdom of God* is the shared subject matter of both Testaments. That kingdom, whose manifestation is so much the subject matter of the Old Testament but is most often discussed with reference to the New Testament, is most fully in view when seen in the light of both Testaments. The proclamation of the *basilea tou theou* is fundamental to the mission of Jesus and the claims of the New Testament, but the political understanding of the realm of God's sovereignty comes from the Old Testament as does the church's understanding of the shape and character of that rule. The Psalms reach their climax in the enthronement psalms (93, 95–99) with the declaration that "the LORD reigns," and the hope of Israel is oriented toward the coming of one who will establish the just and merciful reign of peace that is God's kingdom on earth.[18] The New Testament tells us who this one is while still looking in hope for the full realization of that rule comprehended and expected in both Testaments.

The *Great Commandment*, first set forth in Israel's Torah and then authorized as the summary of the whole by Jesus—consistent with the Jewish tradition that grew out of the Old Testament—offers a profound center around which the whole revolves. The role of the elect as following after no other god but the Lord is articulated in the Shema and then reformulated in Jesus's call to discipleship. Christian living listens to both parts of Scripture to discern what that calling involves. Nor is there anywhere in the Scriptures where this center does not hold, where the Great Commandment does not ground what is said either explicitly or implicitly. That is self-evident in the Law and the Prophets. It is just as much the case for the Writings. In the Psalter, the first commandment is to the fore in all sorts of ways, not least in the significance of trusting in the Lord as the ground of all those human cries inscribed in the psalms of lament.[19] So also for Job the fundamental question is whether Job fears God for nothing. Will he curse God or love God? Here, as in other matters, the Christian community learns not only from its own ongoing story but also from its Jewish brothers and sisters, who know the same command to love the LORD your God as well as your neighbor, and the gift and demand that are both present in that injunction.

---

18. A classic treatment of the theme of the kingdom of God as an expression of the wholeness and coherence of the Old Testament and the New may be found in John Bright, *The Kingdom of God*.

19. For example, Ps 22:4–5 [Heb 5–6].

THE OLD TESTAMENT AND PREACHING

I will make two claims at this point, knowing there is much more that has been and can be said. The first claim is this: *The preaching of the Old Testament is aimed solely at placing upon the minds and hearts of the congregation the claim of the text as the word of God.* What is intended in this assertion is a resistance to more narrow definitions of the aim of preaching from the Old Testament. While all preaching in some way or another seeks to proclaim the gospel in the sense that the sermon should communicate the grace of God upon the believer in a way that calls forth a response of commitment, it is possible to understand this in an unnecessarily restrictive manner, forgetting that the gospel, the good news of God's salvation from sin and suffering, is not sounded first in the New Testament or only heard via the New Testament. The critical point at which such restriction is usually manifest is in the assumption that Old Testament texts cannot be preached properly except as brought into explicit conjunction with the New Testament or with explicitly christological moves.

Texts are always heard *on their own*, that is, in their particularity as the word of God, and also in *two contexts*. One of those contexts is *the whole of Scripture*, so that wherever the text comes from, its resonance with other voices, its place in the complexity of the whole, is in view and may be a part of its proclamation.[20] There is also, however, the context of *the congregation* that receives the word. It is a community of persons shaped and determined by the whole of Scripture. This means that any preaching of an Old Testament text is to those who live and think, pray and praise, listen and question in the light of the whole of Scripture. God's redemptive work in and through Jesus Christ is a given for the faith and life of those who receive the word preached. Where the particular Old Testament text creates resonances that evoke and draw one also into the New Testament word, that is appropriate, and the New Testament word may take its place in the proclamation of the Old Testament text. Often, however the resonances will be self-evident and so clearly implicit that they may be presumed without being articulated because the congregation always hears the proclamation as a community of *Christian* believers.[21]

20. This, of course, is simply an affirmation of the hermeneutical circle as always functioning in the interpretation and proclamation of any specific text.

21. If it is a misunderstanding of the Old Testament as Christian Scripture to assume that it cannot be proclaimed apart from explicit reference to the New Testament or to Jesus Christ, it is equally misguided to insist that the Old Testament be heard only "on its own terms" and without reference to the New Testament.

The second claim about the proclamation of the Old Testament is this: *The Old Testament gives to the church things that tend to be forgotten or diminished when the Old Testament is neglected in its teaching and preaching.* A number of years ago, the New Testament scholar Nils Dahl wrote an essay titled "The Neglected Factor in New Testament Theology."[22] It appeared in a relatively obscure context, a house organ for Yale Divinity School, but still attracted a lot of attention.[23] The "neglected factor" to which Dahl refers is God. While many have responded positively to Dahl's challenge, the point is still noteworthy precisely because of the danger to which it points us. It is possible for much careful and important study of the texts of the New Testament to go on without significant reference to the God whose work in Jesus Christ is the subject matter of the Scriptures. That may not be as large a problem as it might seem *if* the Old Testament and its texts are in constant view and play a large role in the church's proclamation. For it is especially there that the community of faith learns about its Lord. There is no way the church can ignore the God of Israel who is also the Lord of the church if it listens constantly to its Old Testament. From the beginning of the Old Testament to the end, its subject matter is the words and deeds of "the LORD our/your God." Proclamation, therefore, that continually sets the texts of the Old Testament before the people will also keep faith's attention focused on the proper subject of the church's worship: its Lord.

The Old Testament also presents the church with its largest picture of the story of God's work. Even more it keeps before us the realm of God's activity. Some of the resistance to the Old Testament arises because of its very deep immersion in this world in which we live and suffer and die, in which our personal lives are all wrapped up in larger events of national and international affairs. There is an awful lot of killing and war, family conflict and bad behavior of every kind, in the Old Testament. Some of it is quite unpleasant, but it is where the human community lives. The Old Testament touches on every kind of human issue and problem and confronts every kind of theological question. Job's popularity with those for whom the rest of the Scriptures are of little concern is precisely because it confronts the human situation and the question of God so directly. But Job's personal problems and his existential dilemma are only a piece of what the church hears about when it takes up the Old Testament. It also reads about the

22. Dahl, "The Neglected Factor," 3–8.

23. For a recent extensive effort to pick up Dahl's challenge about the neglect of God, see Das and Matera, *The Forgotten God.*

work of God in a people, defined not only by their allegiance to the Lord but by ethnic and historical factors. Neither the work of God nor human response remains on an individual level. They are part of a much larger picture. Indeed, the story is seen from the beginning to be of universal scope, daring to say that what happens in the affairs of people and nations is precisely what God is about.

Central to constant listening to the Old Testament is also an awareness that the work of God is not something to be understood solely in *salvific* terms. God's redemptive activity is everywhere evident, but it is not all that goes on. The divine way of dealing with the reality of sin and wickedness is in terms of election and blessing, the choosing of a people to be the means by which all the peoples of the earth may find blessing rather than curse and judgment.[24] The Old Testament, therefore, not only confronts us with a realistic picture of the context of the Lord's activity in the world; it also enlarges our perception of that work. Human *flourishing* as much as human *redemption* are at the heart of God's intention for this world. Indeed, they are not finally separable features of existence, but the former may get lost in our focus on redemption. The Old Testament holds these together in the paradigmatic story of the exodus from Egypt. At the divine theophany at the burning bush, the Lord begins with these words to Moses:

> I have observed the misery of my people who are in Egypt; I have heard their cry on account of their taskmasters. Indeed, I know their sufferings, and I have come down to deliver them from the Egyptians, and *to bring them up out of that land to a good and broad land, a land flowing with milk and honey*, to the country of the Canaanites, the Hittites, the Amorites, the Perizzites, the Hivites, and the Jebusites. (Exod 3:7–8)

God's salvific work is not only a liberation from the chains that bind us (compare Luke 4:16–21). It is also the gift of new life and blessing. In the profoundest sense possible, the Scriptures of the Old Testament announce that God's offer of life is there for all, that the Lord's intention is that all

24. This assumes that the word and call of the Lord to Abraham are an explicit outgrowth of what has happened in Genesis 1–11, specifically the way in which sin has led to the judgment of curse, and that all that follows after Gen 12:1–4a is an outgrowth of the call and promise of God and Abraham's obedient response. The promise of God is so comprehensive and its stake in a faithful and obedient response from Abraham and his seed so large that the rest of the Abraham story focuses significantly on the issue of that response (for example, Genesis 15 and 22). For the significance of God's blessing for the human story, see Westermann, *Elements of Old Testament Theology*, Parts 1 and 2; and Soulen, *The God of Israel and Christian Theology*, Part 2.

people shall flourish. Such is the good news we hear in Scripture and so belongs always in our proclamation.[25]

25. The argument is not that the New Testament does not know about these things. It knows them and assumes them. But if the New Testament remains the focus of the church's proclamation to the neglect of the Old Testament, it is likely that the complexity and richness of that good news as it has been made known in the fullness of human life and the created order would be diminished and the temptation to reduce the gospel and the Christian message to matters of individual and personal concern alone increased.

THREE

Preaching the Old Testament at Easter

T HE TITLE OF THIS essay would seem to be a kind of oxymoron. In the church's preaching in general, the Old Testament comes out on the short end of the stick. One may properly raise questions about that and criticize the paucity of preaching from the Old Testament. In this instance, however, surely it is justified. If ever there is a moment in the Christian year when the focus of preaching has to be on the New Testament, it is Easter.

While not wanting to argue with such an obvious claim, I would nevertheless suggest there are significant ways, even at Easter, in which the *whole* of Scripture still remains the quarry from which the church's preaching is hewn, and that the Old Testament remains a part of the witness to the power of God that we have come to know especially in the good news of Christ's resurrection from the dead. Justification for keeping the Old Testament in the church's preaching at Easter has at least three grounds:

1. It was specifically to the Old Testament that the church turned to understand who Jesus was and to interpret the passion of Christ. It came to comprehend the meaning of his suffering and death only as it listened carefully to its Scriptures, especially the Psalms and the prophets. One of the side effects of the effort to hear the Old Testament on its own terms has been the dulling of our ears to its powerful prophetic and anticipatory notes.

2. The church's preaching is not necessarily from either the Old Testament or the New Testament but is the preaching of the gospel as found in both contexts. That is no less true at Easter and in its preparation than it is at Advent and Christmas.

3. Jesus's resurrection is an instance, indeed the confirming instance, of the power of God to raise the dead and the testimony that death is not the final or definitive word about our life. The resurrection is, however, just that, and the church must hear in this gospel word the testimony to God's power in our behalf and not become so fascinated by the specifics of the resurrection of Jesus that it forgets that our aim at Easter is to praise the God whose power over death is now made sure and who still lives as Christ with us. It may be that some attending to the Old Testament may take us away from body inspection and tomb excavation and toward the praise of God.

ON THE WAY TO THE CROSS — AND BEYOND

In the early preaching of "the good news about the kingdom of God and the name of Jesus Christ" (Acts 8:12), Philip is sent under divine impetus (an angel and the Spirit) to meet an Ethiopian, apparently a "God-fearer," that is, a Gentile who reads the Scriptures of Israel and worships the Lord. At least that is how he is encountered in this text. The intentionality behind the story is evident; this is not a casual encounter. Not only does the Spirit send Philip into the chariot of the Ethiopian at a very precise moment, but when it is over, the Spirit whisks Philip away. One may presume that the text the Ethiopian is reading is no happenstance either. He is reading from Isaiah 53, specifically verses 7–8, and does not understand what he is reading. More precisely, he has one question. It is the perennial question for readers of this text, from its earliest Jewish interpreters to the most contemporary seminary class of students: of whom does this account of the silent and innocent suffering of one for others speak? Or as the Ethiopian puts it: "About whom does the prophet say this, about himself or about someone else?" What is to be especially noted at this point is what happens next: "Then Philip began to speak, and *starting with this scripture*, he proclaimed to him the good news about Jesus" (Acts 8:35).

Isaiah's account of the Suffering Servant thus becomes the beginning of the proclamation of the good news. One might say that Philip simply grabs the occasion because this was the text that was open. But there is too much self-consciousness and intentionality in this account to allow for that. This is *the* text, the one that opens up the preaching of the gospel. One is compelled, therefore, to ask if there is a lesson for the proclamation of the good news by the church, that it may, and perhaps should, start with the recounting of the Old Testament portrayal of the one who was the Servant of the Lord, and particularly with the account of the suffering, rejection, and final exaltation of this one in whom the will and purpose of the Lord was achieved.

What might, then, be the focus and emphases of such preaching that arose out of the recounting of the work of the Servant in the book of Isaiah?

1. The suffering of the Servant of the Lord, which comes at least in large part at the hands of others, is the *purpose and work of God* ("Yet it was the will/purpose of the LORD to crush him with pain/sickness"). One cannot tell from the prophet's report of the servant what all suffering is meant, but there is no question that it involves at least rejection and oppression by others, and that what happens is at the same time God's clear intention.[1] "The LORD has laid on him the iniquity of us all." The suffering and death of God's servant is a human experience and by human oppression. It is no less the will of God. The Old Testament account of "my servant" in Isaiah 53 is probably clearer and more direct about this than any New Testament interpretation of the death of Jesus.

2. A number of the New Testament texts that quote from or allude to Isaiah 53 do not particularly identify the suffering and death of Jesus as an atoning death.[2] But the extent to which the church hears in this chapter some interpretation of the work of God in and through "my servant" and sees in "my servant" the person and work of Jesus Christ, the will and purpose of God in the suffering and death of the servant is explicitly *God's way of dealing with the reality of human sin*, and the wrongful death of the innocent one is God's way of justifying the sinful many. The perversion that is the judgment of "my servant," who is innocent, becomes God's way of dealing with the sin of the perverted ones, those who "have all turned to our own way" (v. 6). The proclamation of Isaiah 53 serves to keep the church mindful of

---

1. The account of the servant in Isaiah 53 suggests both sickness and deformity as possible indications of the source of the servant's suffering, as well as oppression and apparently death at the hands of others. That the text is poetic and metaphorical, elliptical and ambiguous, means of necessity that one cannot read here a kind of prophecy of the life story of Jesus, though many have been tempted to do so. There are resonances between the passage and the experience of Jesus that lead us to place the two stories in conversation, but one cannot push that conversation too far in its details.

2. In this regard, see the discussion of the explicit quotations from Isaiah 53 and their context in Juel, *Messianic Exegesis*, 119–33.

the meaning of the passion and death of Christ so that it does not lose track of that meaning as it becomes engrossed in the passion play. Isaiah 53 is not itself a significant part of the Passion story; another Old Testament text comes to play there (see below). It is the Isaiah "story" however, that serves to let the church know what is going on "behind the scenes."

3. Isaiah 53 provides a way of understanding the outcome for the many as well as for the innocent one. For the many, and for those who in reading this chapter find themselves among the *we* who speak in its text, that outcome is described as *healing and wholeness or peace*: "upon him was the punishment that made us whole and by his bruises we are healed" (v. 5). That this text should present the outcome so totally in the language of healing and wholeness, of the restoration of peace with God, suggests that such a way of understanding what God has accomplished in the death of Christ is a fruitful way of thinking and talking. Thus preaching that focuses on this subject may want to appropriate some of the same motifs and begin to think about the relationship between forgiveness and healing, between justice or judgment and peace and reconciliation. The Apostle Paul seems to appropriate some of this understanding in one of the places where the language of Isaiah 53 is explicitly in view: ". . . who was handed over to death for our trespasses and raised for our justification. Therefore, since we are justified by faith, we have peace with God through our Lord Jesus Christ" (Rom 4:25–5:1).

4. The New Testament itself sees among the prominent testimonies of Isaiah 53 the word not only about the rejection of "my servant" but also about his vindication and exaltation. So the proclamation of this text should not focus entirely upon the suffering and its rationale but should start and end where the text itself starts and ends, with the exaltation of the servant. Surely this has much to do with the passage that Philip interprets for the Ethiopian as the beginning of the proc-lamation of the good news about Jesus Christ. The passage (53:7–8) concludes, according to the Septuagint, with the words: "For his life is taken away from the earth." This is probably to be understood in this context as a reference to the ascension of Jesus and so to his vindication and exaltation, an understanding of the ultimate fate of "my servant" that is anticipated at the beginning of the account in Isaiah (52:13). The poem about the servant in Isaiah is not simply

about his suffering. It holds the whole story together, and so its proclamation allows one to anticipate the successful accomplishment of the purpose of God through "my servant" and the prospering of the servant without diminishing the depth of suffering that belonged to that accomplishment.

On its way to the cross and beyond, the church listens also to the Psalms and especially to Psalm 22. That is certainly the case in light of the extent to which that text serves in the New Testament to provide the chief interpretive clues to the meaning of the suffering and death of Jesus.[3] But the church's attention to this psalm is itself a reflection of the way in which Psalm 22 serves to model the human situation in extremis and to provide words that portray both the human condition in distress and the joyful expression of praise and thanksgiving that arises when the prayers of the afflicted human being are heard and answered. The quotation of the opening words of the psalm on the lips of Jesus on the cross is the primary point of entry into the psalm because these words make it clear that this one who dies there is not only the servant of the Lord whose suffering is in our behalf. There on the cross is also the one who is not only *for us* ("wounded for our transgressions") but *one of us*, identifying in the moment of suffering with all who find themselves destroyed and oppressed, sick and sorrowing, beset behind and before. The depth of that human experience is surely no more starkly set forth as a sense of divine abandonment than in those opening words. But the appropriation of other verses from this psalm as well as from other laments of the Psalter testify to the way in which Jesus's suffering and death was not simply "foretold" in the psalms but was understood as *embodied* in these outcries. The psalms of lament as primary bearers of the meaning of the suffering and death thus let us know that this suffering of "my servant" was not only God's purpose for dealing with our sins but was also God's work to overcome our suffering. Psalm 22 is about the human predicament. It has to do with God and with others, and experientially it is marked by suffering and oppression, the specific character of which remains open. But it is not explicitly a cry of confession or repentance. It is a cry for God's help in the face of suffering and death. In the New Testament's appropriation of this psalm, we learn that Jesus took upon himself the pain and suffering of human existence, even unto death. The full implications of incarnation are never clearer than in the resonances between this psalm

---

3. For a concise overview of the New Testament quotations of and allusions to this psalm, see Reumann, "Psalm 22 at the Cross."

and the experience of Jesus. Our cry for help, represented in the prayer of Psalm 22, became his prayer for help.

So his vindication became our vindication and the sure word that in Jesus's death God's work to overcome, not only sin, but also suffering and death, has been accomplished. And even as the account of the servant in Isaiah 53 anticipates the vindication and exaltation of the Servant of the Lord, so Psalm 22 holds together in one the terrible suffering of the human being in distress and the marvelous praise and thanksgiving that flow forth when the cry for help has been heard and God has responded and delivered. Both these texts tell the whole story, and that is part of their appropriateness for Easter and the days before.

Drawing on the work of George Steiner, Walter Brueggemann has reminded us of the long Saturday between the darkness and death of Friday and the light and resurrection of Sunday.[4] That is a time of silence and hopelessness. Such silence and hopelessness that are then broken up in surprise and wonder is to be found even in Psalm 22, between verse 21a and verse 21b. We do not know what goes on between the cry, "Save me!" (v. 21a) and the declaration, "you have answered me" (v. 21b). But the silence of that emptiness is where we live and wait.

It may well be that Psalm 22 in its fullness provides the best text for preaching from Good Friday to Easter—the first half of the Psalm providing the text for Good Friday, and the song of thanksgiving in the second part as the Easter text. For Saturday—maybe Psalm 88. Not for preaching, of course—there is no proclamation on Saturday. There is only the incongruity of both waiting and hoping, waiting in hopelessness and hoping in anticipation because we know something. Perhaps the reading of Psalm 88 several times on Saturday will keep us from waiting as if there is nothing at stake, as if three days is only a passing moment, when for those who have truly seen his death it is an eternity.

Praising the God Who Raises from the Dead

Saturday is too soon for the final section of Psalm 22 (vv. 22–31), but that song of thanksgiving become testimony is truly the Old Testament text for Easter. For the proclamation of Easter is from beginning to end the sound of praise and thanksgiving. The proclamation of Psalm 22 as a text

---

4. Brueggemann, *Theology of the Old Testament*, 400–403.

for Easter does at least two things. For one, it is entirely a testimony to the *power of God* that has wrought the deliverance prayed for so poignantly in doubt and trust in the first part of the psalm. If the beginning of Psalm 22 is the explicit voice of the Crucified One, the song of thanksgiving at the end is the implicit voice of the Risen One. In the same manner in which Jesus always pointed to God in his teaching and healing, the song of thanksgiving in Psalm 22 does nothing but call for the praise of God. The only word to be sounded, and the only word to be sounded at Easter, is the final and climactic word of Psalm 22: "He has done it!" (v. 31). The empty tomb is not a witness to Christ; it is a witness to the God who raises from the dead, of which the Christ is the firstborn whose resurrection is the primary testimony to the power of God over death. The church joins with the Risen One bearing witness that "The Lord has done it!" and so we need fear death no longer.

Psalm 22 further suggests that the witness to God's power evoked by this event of deliverance is a witness that goes on and on in time and space. It begins in the congregation, but the ones who praise the God who has answered the cry of the oppressed one extend to "the ends of the earth," to "all the families of the nations" (v. 27). Nor is there any moment when such hallelujahs are not sounded. For those who are already dead in the Lord will bow down and praise the Lord. And "people yet unborn" will come to know this story and respond with their praise and thanksgiving (v. 31).

The particular psalm that has come to the fore in the liturgy of Easter Day functions in a similar way. It is Psalm 118, and its text once more encompasses the whole of the Easter Week experience except that in this instance it is particularly the church's claim about the meaning of Easter that comes to the fore. Several dimensions thus belong to its proclamation:

1. The psalm does not tell a story in quite the same sense as one can perceive in the movement of the servant poem of Isaiah 53 or even of Psalm 22. It moves back and forth from joy to petition, from thanks and exultation to recollection of the terrible trouble and near death. There is not a single direction or a neat logic.

2. The repetition of the opening hymn of thanks (v. 1) again at the end of the psalm (v. 29) serves to set the whole of the psalm as an expression of praise and thanksgiving. All the petition of the psalm, all the references to distress in the psalm are retrospective and now subsumed under the conviction that the Lord "has become my salvation" (v. 14). So "Give thanks to the LORD, for he is good; his steadfast love endures forever."

3.   The deliverance is attested as both individual and communal. There is an *I* who dominates in the song and whose deliverance is recounted in various ways. But there is also a wider group in this psalm, who have themselves cried out (v. 25), and who together rejoice and give thanks. The relationship between the *I* and the *we/us* is not delineated. Both are beneficiaries of God's power and purpose to save. The Easter deliverance is the power of God to redeem the one who died on the cross, but it is also that same power that in Christ now gives life and light (v. 27) to all.

4.   One indication that the passion of Jesus cannot be read into the psalm in an overly simple way is the claim of the *I* of the psalm that "he did not give me over to death." But what is heard even in that assurance, is one of the three central claims of the psalm that surely belong at the heart of its preaching on Easter. That is the exultant cry in verse 17: "I shall not die, but I shall live!" Here the church discerns both the implicit words of the Risen One and the further implication for each one who now, through the resurrection of Christ, is given the words of life. James Mays has marked the sharp contrast between this assertion and the natural human condition:

> The normal human predicament is that, because we must die, the expectation of our final negation infects our living in all kinds of conscious and subliminal ways. The church has found in verse 17 the expression of the transformation worked by the resurrection in one's fundamental stance in life. The way in which believers face every threat and crisis and need is colored by the knowledge that God has not given us over to death. "We whose life is hid with Christ in God ought to meditate on this psalm all the days of our lives, Col 3:3" (Calvin, 4:325).[5]

5.   A further claim of the psalm and one of the main reasons it has come into the Easter life of the community of faith is the announcement that "the stone that the builders rejected has become the chief cornerstone" (v. 22). While the image may simply be a poetic way of talking about startling reversal, it is exactly that unbelievable turnaround that is the good news of Easter. The specific illustration so captures that reality, particularly with its notions of rejection and vindication, indeed exaltation, as the rejected one becomes the head or chief. It is a similar

5. Mays, *Psalms*, 380.

note to what the New Testament writers heard in Isaiah 53. The one now exalted by the power of God was the one rejected in suffering and death at the hands of the world. "The marvelous thing is that the one whom our human instincts and wisdom reject, God has nonetheless, in spite of us and for our salvation, made the chief cornerstone."[6]

6. The final and central claim of the psalm is evident throughout but reaches its peak in verses 23 and 24:

> This is the LORD's doing;
>   It is marvelous in our eyes.
> This is the day that the LORD has made;
>   let us rejoice and be glad in it.

The resurrection is "the LORD's doing." The deliverance wrought that first Easter is God's work. The first and third lines echo each other as do the second and fourth lines. They provide the structure of faith that Easter evokes. The starting point is the claim (vv. 23a and 24a) that on that day the Lord acted. All naturalistic explanations fall before the reality that this is not human work. This is God's doing. The first line of verse 24 is richly ambiguous. We know it primarily as the indicator that Sunday has been given to us by the Lord's marvelous deed of raising Jesus from the dead. By that act the Lord has made this day for us. So every Sunday the church celebrates and gives praise for the wonder of God's victory over death accomplished in and through the resurrection of Jesus. But another translation of this line is equally possible. It echoes the conclusion of Psalm 22 quite precisely: "This is the day the LORD has acted." This is the day the Lord has done it! In such a manner the text points powerfully to the significance of this moment in all of human and cosmic history. This day is not like any other day. This is the day that God has done what could not be done and raised Jesus from the dead.

So then, faith sees what God has done and responds in several ways: It stands in awe and wonder before "the LORD's doing." "It is marvelous in our eyes," say the singers of Psalm 118. The term for "marvelous" (*nipla'ot*) belongs to a stock of words of the same root that Walter Brueggemann has properly translated as "impossible," "too difficult"—or in the nominal form

---

6. Ibid., 381.

impossibilities.[7] It is this word with which the angelic messengers confront old Sarah and, centuries later, young Mary as they announce the birth of a child: "Is anything too difficult (*yippale'*) for the LORD?" It is the same word that Jeremiah hears when he scoffs at being told to buy land in Judah when the Babylonian army is at the gates of Jerusalem: "See, I am the LORD, the God of all flesh; is anything too difficult (*yippale'*) for me?"[8] Brueggemann has rightly noted that such impossibilities becoming possible—births to old women and young virgins, new life in the face of death, and resurrection of the dead—require a new kind of epistemology, a new way of knowing. Where such a new way of knowing is possible, two more things will happen.

The community will sing for joy and shout the praise of God because what has not been has been, what was impossible has happened, death has given way to life. If there is weeping and sorrow and sadness in the days before, the sounds of Easter are only joy and exultation, giving thanks and praising God for what we have seen and heard.

But our joy is not self-contained. It is recounted and told to all who will listen and be drawn into the circle of praise. "I shall not die, but I shall live, *and recount the deeds of the LORD*" (v. 17). The good news of what God has done in raising Jesus from the dead is told and retold. The ripple of praise that begins on Easter Day and extends through time and space carries with it an ongoing and never-ending testimony to what God has done for us.

The wonder and joy and recounting all come together in the church's hymns of praise.

---

7. Brueggemann, "'Impossibility' and Epistemology," 167–88.

8. Jeremiah has assumed that nothing is too difficult for the Lord in his prayer (32:17), but the conclusion of the prayer implicitly undercuts the previous assumption, as indicated by the Lord's response and question back to Jeremiah.

FOUR

Preaching Repentance in a Narcissistic Age: Psalm 51

A s I BEGIN TO write these words, I have just come from the service of Evensong at King's College Chapel in Cambridge. There we heard Psalm 51 sung by the beautiful voices of the deservedly famous King's College Choir. The service was worshipful and uplifting, as it regularly is for me. But I was struck by a sense of tension between that liturgical and musical rendition of Psalm 51 and the profusive *mea culpa, mea culpa, mea maxima culpa* that is implicit in the psalm, a text given to us—according to its superscription—as a prayer that belongs to the acts of covetousness, murder, and adultery by the political leader of the land. I left the Evensong service with a large sense of incongruity and a wonder if this great penitential prayer has lost its edge, if it is possible for it to become a prayer that we wish to pray or need to pray.

Various features of our contemporary life work against Psalm 51 again becoming truthful for us:

1. Focus upon the self is intense in our culture, but it is entirely uplifting and zealously resistant to any negative words about the self. Twenty years ago one of the most popular books among clergy was *I'm OK, You're OK*. It is still very difficult for anyone to say, at least in the moral sphere, I'm not okay, and even less likely that one will risk saying to another, you're not okay.

2. There is a large inclination within us not to take responsibility for our misdeeds and thus not to confess them as sins. That is nothing new. It is as old as the Garden of Eden and that first human response to the first question of moral accountability: "The woman whom you gave

to be with me, she gave me from the tree, and I ate" (Gen 3:12). It is somebody else's fault, or even God's.

But this unwillingness to accept responsibility, to discern and accept moral accountability seems especially acute in our time. There seems to be an increasing tendency to assume or claim that someone else has really brought about the trouble that seems to have our fingerprints on it. That is true not only for ourselves but as we look at others. Obvious cases of brutal crimes may be the exception, but social analysis has taught us to analyze and look for a pattern of causation that reduces blame, that distances personal accountability from the act as the various contributing factors of environment, heredity, temporary insanity, provocation, and the like are uncovered that account for the act in a way that leaves little room for one to say, I have sinned. In the past months, the *New York Times* told of a grandmother who made her granddaughter consume a poison drink that killed her, and the article focused on identifying who in the social agencies did not spot the problem. The moral evil was not named. Blame must be somewhere else—in the structures of society in this instance.

3. The autonomy of the self is not only a post-Kantian dogma but a lived reality for most people in the Western world. In his great study of the modern identity, *The Sources of the Self*, Charles Taylor notes that the cultural turn toward personal fulfillment, which Philip Rieff called "the triumph of the therapeutic," produces modes of life with a kind of shallowness:

> Because no non-anthropocentric good, indeed nothing outside subjective goods, can be allowed to trump self-realization, the very language of morals and politics tends to sink to the relatively colourless subjectivist talk of "values." To find the meaning to us "of our job, social class, family and social roles," we are invited to ask questions like this: "In what ways are our values, goals, and aspirations being invigorated or violated by our present life system? How many parts of our personality can we live out, and what parts are we suppressing? How do we *feel* about our way of living in the world at any given time?" . . . Community affiliations, the solidarities of birth, of marriage, of the family, of the polis, all take second place.[1]

---

1. Taylor, *Sources of the Self*, 519.

T. S. Eliot has identified the modern mentality in another fashion in his play *The Cocktail Party*, when Celia Coplestone says to Sir Henry Harcourt-Reilly, the psychiatrist and soul doctor of the play:

> I've never noticed that immorality
> Was accompanied by a sense of sin:
> At least, I have never come across it.

When asked by him what was the point of view of her family on these matters, she says:

> I had always been taught to disbelieve in sin.
> Oh, I don't mean that it was ever mentioned!
> But anything wrong, from our point of view,
> Was either bad form, or was psychological.[2]

In contemporary society, there is a growing focus on the moral life of prostitutes and celebrities. Whatever may cause our absorption with the behavior patterns of such folk, our tendency is often to view their peccadillos as bad form. Or if the problem of the celebrity moves into the sphere of injustice, the response on the part of the person(s) involved may be one of ignorance of the problem or formality, as when Frank Gifford passed out $100 bills to garment workers who made his wife's line of dresses at very low wages.

Toward the end of his book, Charles Taylor investigates "the search for moral sources *outside* the subject through languages which resonate *within* him or her, the grasping of an order which is inseparably indexed to a personal vision."[3] It is that sense of sources outside oneself that resonate within one that underlies the conviction articulated by the psalmist, whose outcome is a powerful challenge to the self's autonomy because human fulfillment is, in this context, understood to lie in a community ethos both highly relational and shaped by an external reality that has called it into being and given it both blessing and direction, the God against whom *I* have sinned.

Psalm 51 thus presents itself to us as a large challenge and in a double sense. It challenges the common self-understanding of our time, and it challenges the preacher who would set its word abrasively against the contemporary ethos. To take it up, however, may be to offer the congregation a deeper view of the inner self than the bland analyses and therapies of

2. Eliot, *The Complete Poems and Plays*, 361.
3. Taylor, "Sources of the Self," 520.

our time present and, ultimately, to uncover both the truth of our inward selves, our souls, and a mechanism for dealing with that truth. In pursuit of a deeper and more truthful understanding of the human self, the following reflections on Psalm 51 are offered.

1. The psalm is about the terrible reality of sin and what is possible in the face of that reality. One cannot miss the heaping up of vocabulary for sin. The terms "sin," "iniquity," and "transgression" are repeated throughout the psalm.[4] There is no hiding behind euphemistic expressions, no avoidance of the reality that evokes this outcry. Wrong has happened, and the praying one of this psalm (the superscription, of course, says this is David) is acutely aware of that and of his or her accountability, his or her sin/iniquity/transgression. The psalm thus sets itself in a single context, but one with much elasticity. That single context is the unmistakable fact of wrongdoing that not only cannot be denied or suppressed but obviously has taken over the very soul of the wrongdoer.

2. The prayer of a sinner for help that is this psalm, therefore, does not arise out of the sense of a general condition of sin but out of the acute consciousness of real and terrible misdeeds, of specific acts. This is the case despite the apparent depiction of a general and original sense of sin in verse 5 [Heb. v. 7]. While it may be possible to read that verse in such a way, it is more likely that the reference to being conceived and born guilty and sinful is an expression of the depth of the sinner's conviction of sin. The poetic form of this prayer leads one to see here a powerful expression of this overwhelming sense of guilt. The cry of verse 5 is not an analysis of the human situation but the feeling of one whose sense of sin is so great that it seems to have been there always. Such an overwhelming feeling is truthful but not generally descriptive of the human condition.

    That this is the case is reinforced by the superscription, which is given to us as an interpretive indicator of the context in which these words are to be understood. They are the outcry of one who was both a man after God's own heart and an adulterer-murder. This prayer belongs specifically to the occasion of adultery and murder. Generally when the community of Israel, or the individual within that

4. For a discussion of how the poet's pairing of the words for sin achieves a result "in which one is overwhelmed with the poet's sense of sin but not dulled by a monotonous repetition" see Miller, "Studies in Hebrew Word Patterns."

community, confessed sins, the heart of the confession was, as it is here, the words "We/I have sinned," and that acknowledgment regularly referred to a specific act of transgression that has been described in the narrative or the text that leads into the formal confession. It is rare that such a confession is made as a general claim. It is in reference to a quite identifiable act.[5]

One notes further that generally the words for wrongdoing in the psalm are in the singular. While the singular can refer to a broader reality, it suggests primarily the specific sin that has elicited the prayer of confession. There is a repeated plural form, "my transgressions" in verses 1 and 3 (cf. v. 13). When that is seen in relation to the superscription, it suggests that the multiplicity involved is not to be understood as a vague, undifferentiated assortment of sins great and small—"whatever," in the colloquial language of our day. Instead, "my transgressions" are the quite specific, concrete, interacting and interrelated complex of acts around David's taking of Bathsheba: at a minimum, acts of coveting, adultery, and murder, but in fact encompassing also misuse of royal power, sexual assault, conspiracy, and betrayal. The psalm invites us to that searching of the soul that is not content with a superficial acknowledgment of a propensity for sin or sins generally, but with a confession of the very real and often complicated acts that have betrayed and undone another—close at hand or far away.

All of this means that Psalm 51 may not necessarily be preached as always and universally applicable to the congregation but in order to make it available when the soul has truly and specifically sinned and is stricken with that recognition, aware that what one has done is not "bad form" but sin, in fact the conviction to which Celia Coplestone comes in Eliot's play.

3. The problem that sin presents in this text is wholly a problem with God. In apparently stark contrast to the information provided by the superscription, the psalm speaks of a sin that is *only* against the Lord (v. 4). But the disjunction between the superscription and the text is only apparent, not real. The connection of the text to the David and Bathsheba story is precisely through the line "against you, you alone have I sinned" (v. 4a; cf. 2 Sam 12:13) "and done what is evil in your sight" (v. 4a; cf. 2 Sam 12:9). It is in Nathan's judgment speech against

5. Cf. Miller, *They Cried to the Lord*, chap. 7.

David that the sin against Uriah is seen as a despising of the Lord and the word of the Lord (2 Sam 12:9).

The need for repentance rests in the fact that transgression and sin, however heinous the effects on human beings, are at root a terrible violation and disturbance of the person's (or community's) relationship with God. If earlier ages have seemed to overstress the reality of sin and guilt, they have at least done so in the certainty that God grounds our life and it is not self-grounded. The problem of preaching repentance is the problem of preaching about something that assumes theonomous existence when we live under the implicit assumption of autonomous existence. While the Bible knows about human reconciliation when offences are committed against a brother or sister (for example, Genesis 33; 50:15–21), and Jesus's teaching calls for such reconciliation before gifts are brought to the altar, that is, brought to God (Matt 5:21–26), forgiveness in the Old Testament is an act of God because the sin against the neighbor is always more deeply a despising of God.[6]

Preaching repentance, therefore, is different from preaching reconciliation and restitution. The latter is an important human act, fundamental to Christian community. Reconciliation and restitution are also more comprehensible to the modern spirit, which tends to assume that the deepest relationship is with the neighbor and so focuses on mending that relationship.[7] But again, the thrust of Scripture is that reconciliation is fundamentally

---

6. In this connection, see the important work of Shriver, *An Ethic for Enemies*. While I would not see the encounter between Joseph and his brothers as culminating in forgiveness, as does Shriver, his comment on Psalm 51 is very much on target:

> On the surface, to say that David's adultery with Bathsheba was sin against God and God only is to reduce to trivial importance the multiple damages done to human beings in the incident. But the narrative associated with the later psalm (2 Sam 11–12) does not permit such an interpretation: there a child dies, a king suffers public humiliation at the hands of a prophet, and the future of his kingship suffers too. The point of Psalm 51 is that the God of Israel takes its sin more seriously than it does. As with the Greeks and many other religious traditions, God and the gods are protectors of the moral order, springing into actions of judgment and punishment when it suffers violation. But in the Hebrew case, the sense of personal affront to the divine is stronger; the one God of Israel is never on vacation from attentiveness to its sins. (29)

7. Note the centrality of the theme of reconciliation in the Confession of 1967 of the Presbyterian Church (USA).

God's work in Jesus Christ and is God's overcoming the yawning gap in the relation between ourselves and God that our sins have created (2 Cor 5:18).

The problem of preaching repentance, therefore, is in direct proportion to the congregation's conviction that its life really is grounded in God. Without that operative assumption, all talk of sin and repentance is received as anachronistic, a holdover from another time, an archaic "preacherish" way of talking about our problems. Preaching that evokes repentance is prepared for by preaching that confronts the congregation in inescapable ways with the reality of God.

4. Far from being bad form, or a vague acknowledgment of the preacher's claims, the sense of sin articulated by the psalmist is a real and terrible experience. It has shaken the very ground of his or her being. It has taken all joy out of life. It has created a sense of being stained, of being so marked by the sin, that one is dirtied (vv. 2, 7). The sin does not need to be pointed out in this case, or, if we take the David story as an interpretive clue, once pointed out it now overwhelms the sinner. The sin is real, and its reality is doing in the psalmist. No lament against enemies and oppression carries any more pleading and beseeching tone than does this one. Look at the verbs: "have mercy," "blot out," "wash me," "cleanse me," "purge me," "wash me," "let me hear joy," "hide your face," "create, put a new spirit," "do not cast away," "do not take," "restore," "sustain," and "deliver." The depth of the psalmist's awareness of his sin is matched only by the sense of need it has created. As much as any lament, this psalm is a cry for help. This person is undone as much as any speaker in the psalms. The destruction of this soul, however, is not by any external forces. It is by the terrible weight of the committed sin and the way it stares him in the face constantly. And so the psalmist cries out in desperation. Here is no intoned general confession of sins we never thought of until we read them out loud from the church bulletin. This is trauma, desperation, a terrible burden that must be lifted.

5. It is the prophetic preaching of Nathan, however, that opens David's eyes. That context suggests to us there is a role for the preaching of the word that may, as indirectly as Nathan's parable about the poor man's lamb, create the ground for an apprehension of sin on the part of the congregation. The reading and interpretation of the psalm may break through the self-protecting veneer to allow the *mea culpa* to come

forth when it has not, when the sin is really there but buried beneath or covered over by the veneer.

Such preaching will carry with it the learning of this psalm, that the transformation of the soul and spirit, the cleansing from the sense of stain—a powerful image not to be easily discarded as an outdated way of speaking—is God's act. If this psalm is a powerful confession of sin, it is more radically a fall upon the grace of God. The imperatives listed above make one aware that repentance in this psalm is not a merely human act. Indeed, repentance here is only implicit though very real. The focus of this psalm is on the plea for God's grace and compassion. It is Israel's oldest confession of faith that the God it worships is merciful, compassionate, and full of steadfast love (Exod 34:7). That is the starting point of this psalm in verse 1. It is the way out for the sinner who is overwhelmed by the weight of the wrong that she has done. For Celia Coplestone, the way out was an act of atonement. The word of the gospel confirms that, but it is an act that has already happened and demonstrated the bent of God to be merciful, gracious, and compassionate—even before the worst of our sins. Thus, the critical word of the preacher is not only in the sermon. There is no more significant act in the service of worship than the assurance to the congregation: "Your sins are forgiven." Those words are never said casually. If they are really true, then they have the capacity to turn the trauma of sin into the healing of redemption, the desperation of one convicted into the hope of one released. As they declare the reality of God's grace, no burden remains too large to let go, and no stained heart that the Lord cannot wash clean.

FIVE

Preaching the Ten Commandments

WITHOUT ANY CONCRETE DATA to support it, my hunch is that the degree of preaching of the Ten Commandments is in inverse proportion to the degree of cultural interest in them. That is, the Commandments are widely a part of the political and cultural scene but less clearly the subject of proclamation or evident in the liturgy of the church. They are an icon or a potential icon, but that role seems to have been taken over by sociopolitical uses of the Commandments more than by religious expressions. There are still churches that have the Commandments in some public place, but they are probably not as numerous as those churches that have the national flag prominently displayed in the sanctuary. Meanwhile, outside the churches there are strong movements to have the Commandments prominently and conspicuously present in schools, courtrooms, legislatures, and post offices. Zeal for the transformation of the Commandments from a religious directive to a cultural icon whose public display is believed to have potential for changing public behavior, is very much on the part of religious persons, who have a hunch that these fundamental guidelines for behavior that arise out of the story of a particular community of faith have a public significance and should not be confined to the religious or cultic spheres.

Perhaps they are on to something. Or it may be that our conversation about and attention to the Commandments has fixed itself on questions of the public function of the Commandments, their place in civil society versus their restriction to the community of faith, because the Commandments have become a given in the life of the church, but not a given that presses for much discussion or interpretation. Within the Reformed tradition as well as the Lutheran, such inattention is a little surprising. The interpretation of the Commandments is a central part of the catechetical tradition, reaching back to earliest stages of the *Didache* and the church fathers and becoming prominent already in Augustine's catechesis.

Our tendency to assume the givenness and obviousness of the Commandments without much elaboration probably is rooted in various realities. We take the Commandments for granted in the church and so assume their importance without talking about them. At the same time, there are many persons who find the Commandments reductionistic as an approach to dealing with moral issues of any significance. That is, they are too simple to give much help beyond the very basic issues. What they deal with are moral verities that are so accepted that they do not need serious discussion. Where they need to be lifted up is in those segments of society or those situations and circumstances where they do not seem to be operative. Presumably church people have and know the Commandments, so nothing more needs to be said there except to reaffirm the obvious to which all are agreed. The knotty matters of moral decision making and acting cannot be dealt with simply on the basis of the Commandments. Thus such hot topics as abortion or homosexuality are not subject to scrutiny via the Commandments either because what they have to say is so obvious and uncomplicated (for example, do not kill), or because they simply do not address the crucial issue and so cannot be of much help. Still others, within the community of faith and without, object to the negative and obligatory character of the Commandments that seems to brook no qualification and couches theological and ethical matters in largely prohibitive terms. They place obligations without taking account of situations and presenting factors. When Joseph Fletcher wrote his famous little book *Situation Ethics* a generation ago, he took particular aim at some of the Commandments and their failure to deal with the complexities of moral decision and asserted as their subservience to or replacement of an ethic of love.

A RECOVERY OF TEACHING AND PREACHING

If any of this be true, then what are we to do with the Commandments? At least one avenue worth considering is the church's recovery of a tradition of teaching and preaching the Commandments.[1] There are several reasons for this, some of them quite pragmatic:

1. A useful and classic example of the tradition of preaching the Commandments is *John Calvin's Sermons on the Ten Commandments*. The sermons are preached on the basis of the Deuteronomic form of the Commandments.

- The Commandments are not self-evident and self-interpreting. Their simplicity should not disguise the need of the church to clarify their meaning and force and instill their practice through its preaching and liturgy, indeed through the practice of the whole of its life.

- The familiarity of the text invites the hearer into thinking about the known and accepted in a fresh way. The point of such preaching is not the novelty of the text but exploration in a deeper way into that which the congregation presumes to know easily.

- Preaching the Commandments keeps the proclamation rooted in the biblical text, but it now engages also that which has its place as doctrine and teaching. So preaching in this instance is not directed by the lectionary but by the catechisms of the church.

- Theology and ethics are thus pushed to the front of the preaching enterprise by the very nature of the material.

- The nature of the material also creates the possibility of an extended series of teaching or preaching occasions in which the congregation knows what to expect and can anticipate and the preacher/teacher has a plan for a prolonged study given to her by the text itself. Whether this means ten sermons or lesson plans, fewer than ten, or more than ten remains to be decided by the preacher or teacher. But any serious engagement with this text in either its Exodus or Deuteronomic form will have to involve a number of sermons or lessons. One of the problems with staying with the lectionary at this point is that the Commandments come there only as a whole and as the basis for a single Sunday. It is hard to conceive of doing fewer than ten sermons because of the congregation's expectation, created by the text and their familiarity with its content, and it is more likely that one will do somewhat more than that.

What is being suggested in the rationales offered above does not mean that one cannot preach a single sermon on the Commandments as a whole or a sermon on one of the Commandments apart from treating the whole. That is, the moral and theological issues of the commandments, whether they have to do with the nature and value of human life, truth telling, Sabbath observance, or the like, are large enough that one may quite well take up one of these issues on the basis of the appropriate Commandment(s) without having to go on and teach or preach on all of them. And even a prolonged series of sermons on the Commandments would probably need to take one occasion to think about them as a whole.

There is need, however, for a *strategy of preaching* and one that recognizes the comprehensive character of the Commandments that tends to impose certain directions on how we take them up. It may be that one will want, either at the beginning or perhaps as a conclusion to preaching the Commandments, to take up the character of the Commandments as *law* or the issues of the *place of the law* in the Christian life. Reformed Christians have tended to see the Commandments especially in relation to the third use of the law as a guide for the sanctified life.[2] While Luther did not develop a so-called third use, he saw in the Commandments both a form of natural law manifesting God's moral will for a fallen humanity and also, with Paul, the practice of God's love command by the Christian. He also saw how the Scriptures in a broad way provide the rich interpretive exposition of the Commandments: "Now Paul shows beautifully on the basis of the Decalogue what it means to be a servant through love . . . All the admonitions of the prophets in the Old Testament, as well as of Christ and the Apostles in the New Testament, concerning a godly life, are excellent sermons on and expositions of the Ten Commandments."[3] It is out of just such a conviction that Luther could say, as he did in the Preface to his *Large Catechism*, "Anyone who knows the Ten Commandments perfectly knows the entire Scriptures."

Luther and Calvin offer a shared way into the Commandments, one that is present in the later confessions and may be central for the preaching of the Commandments. For Luther this way is perhaps best exemplified in his interpretation of the First Commandment: The *negative* of the Commandment prohibiting the worship of other gods is really a matter of the *positive* placing of one's trust wholly in God. More self-consciously hermeneutical, Calvin suggested a method of approach to the interpretation of the Commandments in which he drew on the familiar figurative approach known as synechdoche, that is, seeing a larger whole in the smaller part, a larger meaning in the specific and seemingly confined Commandment,

2. Calvin's treatment of the uses of the law and of the Commandments may be found in book 2 of his *Institutes* as well as at the end of his commentary on the law in his *Harmony of the Pentateuch*.

3. The quotation is from Luther's *Lectures on Galatians*. Other places where Luther takes up the Commandments in an extensive way are his *Small Catechism*, *Large Catechism*, and his *Treatise on Good Works*. For a very helpful comparison of Calvin and Luther on the law, see the essay by Dowey, "Law in Luther and Calvin."

what I would call a trajectory of meaning flowing out of the particular Commandments. Calvin's approach may be suggestive for preaching on particular commandments. He proposed a three-part approach: examine the *subject* of each commandment: that is, what it is talking about; ask after the *end* of each Commandment, that is: what it indicates to us is either pleasing or displeasing to the one who gives the law; and develop an argument from the Commandment to its *opposite*. In this last move, Calvin suggested we discern the positive obligation that flows from a negative command and the prohibition that may be implicit in the positive commands (sometimes even explicit as in the "do not work" dimension of the "observe the Sabbath"). In Calvin's terms, "an injunction of any thing good is a prohibition of the opposite evil . . . a prohibition of crimes is a command to practise the contrary duties." So the interpretive and preaching task is to help the congregation see both aspects of the Commandment's force, its positive and its negative, its *dos* as well as its *don'ts*.[4]

Any preaching of the Commandments will find in such a proposal a way into the Commandments that opens them up and moves from reductionistic and negative interpretations to rich and complex ways the Commandments create an ethic of love for the Christian. Thus the commandment not to steal unfolds an ethic of neighbor love that has to do not only with making sure that one does not illegally and stealthily take what belongs to one's neighbor but also with protecting the goods of one's neighbor, being available for safekeeping of the property of another, and avoiding legal acts that endanger the economic well-being of the neighbor.

Preaching the Commandments probably involves some effort to lay out the *ground* for the ethics of the Commandments. The Prologue offers the best entrée into that subject. It is easy to get hung up on whether the Commandments are duty or response, obligations laid upon us or grateful response to our redemption and freedom in Christ. The Prologue to the Commandments (Exod 20:2//Deut 5:6) suggests that this is a false distinction. Or to put it another way, the Prologue may help us understand the distinction properly. The Commandments come in the form of command or prohibition, placing certain obligations or duties upon those who hear and receive them. So the first hearers responded to the word: "Everything that the LORD has spoken we will do" (Exod 19:8). Living in obedience to

---

4. The Reformed confessions and Luther's *Large Catechism* are helpful in seeing the details of both positive and negative specifics that are implicit in the particular commandments.

the expressed word of the Lord is incumbent upon the community that receives the Commandments. But the Prologue lets us know that such obligations grow out of the gracious and redeeming love of God that has set this people free. Because "I am the LORD your God who brought you out of the land of Egypt, out of the house of slavery, you shall have no other gods before me," and so forth. The acceptance of the obligations is an expression of deep gratitude, and the stipulations provide a way of living under the rule of the one who has set us free. The covenantal structure in which the Commandments are to be understood makes this clear.[5] The covenant begins in the gracious acts of God for the people, by which God becomes their and our God. It is completed in the response of the people to live as God wills them and us to live, which is the way in which they and we become the people of God. Is that obligation or gratitude? It is both, and the Reformed confessions confirm that. Take, for example, the Geneva Catechism, Question #139:

> M. *Why does He mention this at the beginning of His law?*
>
> C. To remind us how much we are bound to obey His good pleasure, and what ingratitude it would be on our part if we do the contrary.

The Heidelberg Catechism places the Decalogue under the rubric "Thankfulness" and sees in it an explanation of "what *gratitude* I *owe* to God for such redemption" (Question 1—italics added).

Out of all these hints and guidelines from the tradition, one may develop a comprehensive approach to the preaching of the Commandments. Thus, they may be seen as a fulsome response to the question that each Christian, consciously and subconsciously, asks: *How then shall we live?* The Commandments present themselves as guidelines and directions for the Christian life, and preaching them may be shaped to raise and respond to that question at every point. If that is the case, one may want especially to look at the Deuteronomic version of the Decalogue (Deuteronomy 5) and the way in which the chapters before and after the preaching of the law (Deuteronomy 1–4 and 29–30) set the offer of life as God's good gift to the people and see the law as the means and the way to the good life and to God's blessing (for example, Deut 30:15–20).

Another possibility of framing the preaching of the Commandments that arises out of the tradition but is expressed here in the language of Paul

---

5. In Deut 4:13, the "covenant" is defined as "the ten words/commandments."

Lehmann is an interpretation of them as "*a primer for learning to spell, and especially to spell out freedom.*"[6] Here, one will help the congregation find in the Commandments an understanding of that service that is perfect freedom. The preacher may want to set the Commandments in the context of the Exodus story and what the Lord tells Moses to give to Pharaoh as a reason for letting the people go out. It is that "they may worship/serve me" (Exod 7:16; 8:2; 9:2; 10:3).[7] As the story makes very clear, such service is the way of freedom from human tyrannies that oppress. True freedom is in the service of God. What does that mean or imply? The Commandments help us figure out that freedom/service. They teach us how to spell and especially how to spell *freedom*.

An alternative strategy might be to set the preaching of the Commandments *in terms of the Great Commandment* so that one sees all the details of the Commandments as an articulation and spelling out of what it means to love God and to love the neighbor. These by themselves are very general notions. What is the content of loving God? What is the way I love my neighbor other than having a generalized good feeling about those around me and trying not to do anything bad to them? Is it possible to be more specific about loving God? How is that demonstrated quite concretely? The Commandments are not the last word on this, but they are the primary specification of what such love of God and love of neighbor are all about, as Paul says in Rom 13:8–10.

A not dissimilar way into the Commandments is to try to lay out the way in which they provide the marks for *the good neighborhood*. Here the image is one of moral space, and the preacher's aim is to show how the Commandments fill up that space, making the neighborhood a good place to live. Such an understanding can be placed in relation to a similar image that permeates the psalms in their depictions of what God has done to deliver and set free those who are oppressed or suffer in some fashion. Often one hears that God has set the suffering one in a broad place (e.g., Pss 4:1; 18:19; 31:8; 118:5). The freedom is a kind of elbow room for the one who felt hemmed in, drowning, caught in a net. Now how does one live in the broad place of God's freedom? That is what the good neighborhood is all

---

6. Lehmann, *The Decalogue and a Human Future*, 5 (italics original).

7. The verb *'abad* means both "worship" and "serve." The coincidence of meaning is, of course, critically important in understanding what is meant. The service of God and the worship of God are one and the same, and the Commandments have their locus in the service/worship of God and so are expressions of a single reality experienced in various ways: liturgically, ethically, politically, and the like.

about, and the Commandments are the neighborhood rules. As they are operative in the lives of the neighbors, the neighborhood, however large or small, really is a better place to live.

Two Approaches

Whatever the overall rubric or framework for directing one's preaching the Commandments, two particular moves can be helpful in preaching the individual commandments. One is to *investigate the ways in which the law codes of the Old Testament give some specification, elaboration, and illustration of what the generalized and nonspecific Commandments are after.* Looking at these other texts is not a simple operation and so will demand some time on the part of the preacher. Pay particular attention to the specific cases or laws in the Book of the Covenant (Exodus 21–23), the Deuteronomic Code (Deuteronomy 12–26), and the Holiness Code (Leviticus 17–26). In these bodies of law—the statutes and ordinances—many of the kinds of issues and cases that grow out of the basic guidelines of the Commandments are set forth. It has been suggested that the Deuteronomic Code has been ordered according to the sequence of the Decalogue. That proposal has some plausibility, but it is not always clear exactly which specific statutes and ordinances fit which Commandment, even if one is moving through the Code with the sequence of the Commandments in mind. Nevertheless, the very possibility of working this out is heuristic as it suggests that we look in these ancient cases for how Israel worked out the details of its obedient response to God embodied in the ten words, the covenant (Deut 4:13). For example, when one looks at Exod 21:16, one discovers that the prohibition against stealing was first aimed at the stealing of a person, what we call kidnapping. Further, in that same context, it is clear that the purpose of the theft is economic gain at the expense of the freedom of the neighbor. The interrelationship between slavery, theft, and economic issues begins to unfold in this particular case. Then, as one looks at Exod 22:1ff., where theft is explicitly the topic, one discovers there is a particular concern in these specific cases for theft of the means of production, the work animals of the neighbor. In the Deuteronomic Code, the section that would seem to correspond with the commandment to honor parents has to do with various officials in the public life of the community: elders, prophets, priests, the king. Here is the basis for the tradition's finding in this commandment some direction about how we are to relate to various kinds of authorities—beginning with parents but extending to others who have some proper role over us. Or a look at Deuteronomy 15 in relation to the Sabbath commandment helps to see in that commandment the beginning of a large sabbatical principle that suggests there may be all sorts of ways in which economic bondage is broken open when the Commandments are directive of the community's life.

The examples above only intimate the large possibilities for drawing upon the Scripture itself for clarifying and interpreting the Commandments. One obviously may move into the teaching of Jesus for further specification of the force of particular commandments. Further, the fact that there is seen to be a stream of interpretive tradition from one time to another helping the community determine in each time and place how the Commandments function as direction for life suggests that this stream continues on into new times and places, including our own. The specification and particularizing of the Commandments is not confined to referencing backwards. There is also the interpretive task of determining in the present moment specific ways and illustrative cases that help us understand how we live in freedom and service through the Commandments. The presence in the Bible of a changing and developing legal and moral tradition out of the Commandments is an implicit authorization for that to continue in our own time.

There is another way in which Scripture provides food for the homiletical enterprise of preaching the Commandments. That is in the *stories* of Scripture as illustration of the force of the Commandments. The stories not only make concrete the way a particular commandment is to be appropriated; they also give some context, show the way in which circumstances affect the obedience to a commandment, and indicate outcomes and consequences when the Commandments are in play or, as is often the case, not in play. The stories are most often of disobedience, for example, the stories of the theft of Joseph by his brothers (Gen 40:15), David's coveting and committing adultery (2 Samuel 11–12), Ahab's coveting of the vegetable garden of Naboth and the subsequent acts of false witness, murder, and theft (1 Kings 21), and Jeremiah's general indictment of the community for violation of the Commandments (for example, Jeremiah 7). From such stories, which may also include prophetic indictments and psalmic narrative laments, one learns something about the way in which life and death are the outcomes of the way persons respond to the Commandments, and we perceive the seriousness of covenantal existence.

SUGGESTIONS

Finally, here are a few simple suggestions for working on particular commandments:

- investigate the various possibilities inherent in the Hebrew expression translated in the NRSV as "before me" and what they may suggest about the way in which other loyalties may compete with one's ultimate loyalty;

- note how the question of idolatry becomes more prominent in those numerations of the Commandments that separate having other gods from making and worshiping images;

- ask what difference it makes whether the images are of other objects of devotion or of the God we worship, and what kinds of images seduce us from the true worship of God;

- note the negative and positive dimensions of the jealousy of God, the positive ones more often denoted by God's "zeal" rather than jealousy;

- ask yourself what's in a name and what mischief is possible with the name of God in personal and corporate life;

- pay attention to the purpose of the Sabbath command in the Deuteronomic form: provision of rest for those who cannot gain it for themselves or without the effort of others to secure it for them ("your male and female slave who are like yourself");

- note the starting point of honoring parents in the way in which adult children treat their aged parents, a starting point that is not the last word in the trajectory of the commandment, as Paul reminds us (Eph 6:1–9);

- wrestle with the restrictions and openness of the term that is sometimes translated "kill" and sometimes "commit murder," avoiding an overly simple resolution in either direction but attentive to the church's tradition on this commandment;

- ask where the neighbor is in the commandment against adultery;

- start with the courtroom and the significance of false and true witness there, and then see if there is something here about lying in a more general way;

- see how the Exodus and Deuteronomic forms of the commandment against coveting serve to suggest categories of things that "belong" to us (and so push us to ask how that belonging works), and also point us to both external acts and internal attitudes as outcomes of coveting;

- do not be suckered into thinking that coveting and theft are prohibitions primarily aimed at the have-nots, who surely are the ones who want their neighbor's property and move to take it! If you think that is the case, read the stories mentioned above a little more carefully.

SIX

Preaching the First Commandment in a Pluralistic World

THE DECISION TO PREACH on the first commandment comes immediately on the question, *What is the first commandment?* That would
seem to be self-evident, and to a large degree it is. Nearly all numerations
of the Commandments understand the first commandment to include
and center in the prohibition: "You shall have no other gods before me"
(Exod 20:3; Deut 5:7), and that is what most people think of when they
hear reference to "the first commandment." The matter, however, is more
complicated than that, and there are numerations of the Commandments
that give a different interpretation of what is the first commandment. In the
Jewish tradition, the first commandment is what others call the Prologue;
that is, the opening verse: "I am the LORD your God who brought you out
of the land of Egypt, out of the house of slavery" (Exod 20:2; Deut 5:6). The
prohibition of other gods is then joined with the prohibition of making
and worshipping images as the second commandment of the Decalogue.
Yet another tradition, represented in the Catholic and Lutheran churches,
understands the first commandment to begin with the prohibition of other
gods but, like the Jewish numeration, includes the prohibition of the images
as part of that commandment and not distinct from it, as in the Reformed
numeration.

The differences here are not simply matters of arbitrary choice about
how to distinguish and number the different commandments. There are
aspects of the text that allow one to read them in different relationships
and including different numerations. Even the Jewish interpretation of the
Prologue as the "first commandment," which would seem to have little justification in light of its character as a divine self-presentation rather than

an injunction or command, can be justified when one remembers that the Bible itself speaks of this group of ten instructions as "the ten words" (Exod 34:28; Deut 4:13; 10:4) not "ten commandments." The first of the "words" is the divine address, "I am the LORD your God . . ." The Reformed differentiation between having other gods and making and worshiping images is fully justified by the recognition that one may have many gods but not images or representations of them and also that one may have only one god but worship that god via physical representations. There are two issues here. At the same time, any interpreter of the text must acknowledge the syntactical point that the plural "them" of "you shall not bow down to them or worship them" has no plural antecedent in the text other than "other gods" in the preceding verse, and that elsewhere the object of "bow down and worship" is most often "other gods," not images.

All of this is to say that preaching the first commandment should pay attention to the tradition of the preacher and the congregation while also being aware that the other numerations suggest there are important relationships here as well as distinctions that may need to be taken account of in the preaching. Interpretation and communication both may wish to take these other perspectives into account. For example, this writer interprets and preaches out of the Reformed tradition and so thinks of the first commandment as the prohibition of other gods. But that is not to be done without awareness of what grounds that prohibition. Some natural law might be brought forward to insist on the oneness of God and of human worship of God, but that is not what comes forth from the Decalogue. There the call to the worship of "the LORD your God" alone and the rejection of all other gods is thoroughly rooted in the preceding verse and the story it encapsulates. That is, the rejection of other gods is because you have been redeemed and delivered by this God and so are under the rule and claim of "the LORD your other God." The point is logical, but it is not the logic of "God can only be one" and so since there are not other gods, one may not worship other gods or turn things into other gods. The logic here is, this is the God who has delivered you and now claims your obedience exclusively and fully. The Decalogue assumes a pluralistic religious world and a plurality of the gods. The exclusive worship commanded is of "the LORD your God." Who is that? To get an answer to that question, see the first verse and read the story out of which it comes, beginning with Exodus 3 and carrying on to Exodus 15. Then go on reading further in your Scriptures and learn more about this one who has delivered you and claimed your full and exclusive devotion.

From these observations at least three implications arise about the connection to the first verse of the Decalogue for the preaching of the first commandment:

First, the Jewish insistence on calling the Prologue the first of the commandments/words is a reminder that all that follows, and especially the prohibition of other gods "before me," is totally grounded in the story of God's deliverance and redemption. The Jewish reading of the commandments in effect inserts a "therefore" between verses 1 and 2 in Exodus 20. It thus grounds all the claims of the commandments in this declaration "I am the LORD your God," but that is especially true of what others of us call the first commandment: the insistence that you may not have other gods. The one we worship is the God who is known by the words and deeds recounted in Scripture—Old Testament and New—and experienced in our own life in the community of faith. In an odd sort of way the modern world has brought us back to the pluralistic cultural reality that was the setting of Scripture, where there were many claims on worship, many religious systems and not some vague generality of deity. To encounter that modern reality through the Commandments, however, is to be highly conscious of the fact that the prohibition of other gods implies the worship of one who is known and revealed in specific character and mode and is not an abstraction whose definition is given in some philosophical or logically derived definition of deity.

The second implication is already present in the first. It is simply that preaching the first commandment is not to be done by way of preaching monotheism. Going about it that way is to argue, there is only one God, so we must worship that one God. The commandment is turned into a logical premise and no longer places any weight upon those addressed, any claim upon them, any sense of genuine danger in its disobedience. Monotheism is largely a modern construct and belongs more to the language of philosophy and history of religions than to preaching. There is much contemporary discussion about the dangers of monotheism and its tendency to violence. As Rodney Stark has shown, the picture is mixed in regard to the effects of "monotheistic religions"; but whether or not, that is not the avenue of preaching.[1] The beginning of the preaching of the first commandment is not, there is only one God, but "I am the LORD your God . . . , therefore you shall have no other gods before me." It is the logic of redemption, not

---

1. Stark, *For the Glory of God.*

the logic of abstraction. We worship the Lord our God not because it is the rational thing to do, but because we are both grateful and commanded.

Third, the preaching of the first commandment on the basis of the claim that precedes it is to preach the commandment as gospel. That does not mean it is not law. It is indeed torah, instruction about how those who have been delivered are to live in this world. But it is about life under grace, and the preaching of the commandment in reference to the divine declaration means that one hears the instruction only as a response to the goodness of God. That is why the story is told again and again, as a reminder of why we live this way.

The first commandment is both gospel and law also in that it not only arises out of being freed but it, in turn, is a freeing word. That is, one is released from obligation, loyalty, and obedience to any other ultimate frame of reference. All other demands and loyalties are penultimate, secondary to the one claim that undergirds all that we do. Such freedom and its sense may result in martyrdom when others seek to make ultimate claims. But that is not the only outcome. If one has no other gods, then all the conflicts and tensions that beset human existence—and they really do—are in some way relegated. They are not finally in control of our lives. We cannot get rid of such tensions and claims on our lives, but we hear that we are free to love and not to bow before other powers.

It is at this point, of course, that one's preaching of the commandment to have no other gods takes some account of the God you have. Obedience is rendered to the one who is this way, that is, whose character is reflected in the story, in the tradition of God's ways and deeds among us. Once more, what frees us is not an abstract absolute but the God who hears the cries of the oppressed, who seeks *shalom* for all, who calls for both justice and holiness among those who serve the Lord. The commitment required by the first commandment is a commitment to One who shows a particular way in the world. To have no other gods is at least to reject any other way than the one identified in the words and acts and instructions of the Lord your God.

If the preaching of the first commandment attends to its connection to what precedes, it also is accountable to what follows. The separation of making and worshiping images from having other gods, as is done in the Reformed tradition, serves to lift up the particular problem or danger of images as a part of one's worship. Subsuming that under having other gods may serve to play down the danger, but it does draw the image issue into the fundamental claim of the first commandment. That is, the images we make may become other gods, even if they are images of the God we have. The iconic is always in danger of becoming the idol. Images and physical representations per se are not a problem. What happens is that the visual and visible and thus tangible may claim our attention so fully that it stands in the place of the Lord your God. It is quite likely that the first target of the commandment against images was the image of the Lord. Deuteronomy 4 is a powerful sermon itself on this commandment, warning against assuming that the one who speaks from heaven, who speaks but is not seen, whose voice comes out of flaming fire that cannot be made, controlled, handled, or touched, is not to be contained in, revealed in, or captured in any physical form that might become an object of devotion. It is important to remember that the commandment is not simply against images. It is against the divinizing of images by not only making them but worshipping them. The other gods you may not have include those forms in which you seek to depict and portray the God you have. The propensity for such representation is large. The giving of the commandments is followed very shortly by the story of the Golden Calf, and the eager need of the people to have something they can see and touch, something tangible to which they can look for guidance. Biblical emphasis on the "word" is precisely a safeguard against turning the relative into the absolute. Even the word, however, may be absolutized. Theological images may become so fixed that they serve to represent God for us. The second commandment is a form of the Protestant principle that nothing can stand in the place of the God who has freed us and now requires our full obedience—no images, pictures, theological systems, languages, or whatever.

The discussion to this point has been an effort to say that preaching the first commandment takes account of its context, not because it is a principle of interpretation that we take account of literary context but because in this instance what precedes and follows the command to have no other gods is an important part of what that command is about. Now one may go on to make some more specific suggestions about preaching the commandment against having other gods:

1. Do not try to solve the problem of the world's different religions and what Christianity should do about them via the first commandment. Take a clue from Deuteronomy. There are other things God is doing, but that is not your business according to Moses's instruction of the people. Deuteronomy may be the book of the Bible most insistent on the first commandment. Chapters 4–11 are a virtual Mosaic sermon

on the first commandment (including the claim of the Prologue and the prohibition of making and worshiping images). Deuteronomy is also the one book that most explicitly suggests that the Lord may have other stories with other peoples: "You," however, you who are addressed by this commandment, are accountable only to the Lord your God and may not involve yourself in anything other than the true and full worship of the Lord your God. There are several acknowledgments of the "other gods" in Deuteronomy. Perhaps indicative of its perspective is Deut 4:19–20:

> And when you look up to the sky and behold the sun and the moon and the stars, the whole heavenly host, you must not be lured into bowing down to them or serving them. These the LORD your God allotted to other peoples everywhere under heaven; but you the LORD took and brought out of Egypt, that iron blast furnace, to be His very own people, as is now the case. (NJPS translation)

Here there is an unelaborated acknowledgment of the presence of other gods in the world, other potential objects of one's worship.[2] Two things are said about them: a) These are allotted by the Lord your God to other peoples; and b) You are to have nothing to do with them because you are the people of the Lord your God. The book of the Bible with the strongest exposition of the first commandment is the clearest place where the other religions are recognized but placed under the domain of the Lord your God. That recognition, however, takes place in the midst of the strongest exposition of the claim of the first commandment that you are to have nothing to do with other gods. There is an acknowledgment of the religious world; indeed, it is a part of what God is about in the universe. But that world is not open to you. Preaching of the first commandment has to live in this tension, both open and closed.[3]

2. Preach the first commandment in both its negative and its positive forms. The commandment has a double function. It points away from those objects of desire and those claims within culture and experience that we might tend to set as centers of meaning and control in our lives. It warns us against thinking there is any aspect of our life, in the

---

2. Cf. Deut 29:24–27 [Heb. 23–26] and 32:7–9.

3. For more extensive elaboration of this point, see Miller, "God's Other Stories."

small sense of our individual existence and in the larger context of our communal and public life, that can exercise final claim on us. The very existence of the negative form is a constant reminder that it is possible to serve other gods. In simple form Jesus warns about this in his declaration, "You cannot serve God and Mammon" (Matt 6:24; Luke 16:13). The negative reminds us of the existence of genuine alternatives, of things in this world that may claim—and receive—our final commitment and trust. Preaching the commandment will seek out, in the life of the congregation, those powers that are both threatening and enticing, those attractions that lure the Christian's turn from the Lord your God to commitments of other sorts. The plural "other *gods*" reminds us that there may be a lot of candidates out there. They start with the economic and political gods—and they may not go any farther than that.

If the prohibitive form of the commandment is a guard against drifting toward the claim of other powers upon us, the positive form of the commandment takes up the "me" of "before me" and points us toward the proper commitment to the Lord our God. There are many positive expressions of the first commandment. The one that stands to the fore and in some sense embodies all the rest is the Shema: "Hear, O Israel, the LORD is your God, the Lord alone. So you shall love the LORD your God with all your heart and with all your soul and with all your might" (Deut 6:4–5). In this manifestation, the positive form of the first commandment underscores two things that belong to its preaching. One is the *character of the relationship*. It is called love, that is, care, affection, and commitment of a sort that can only be described with the human language of love.[4] Giving over of oneself in full devotion to the other is what love is; and that is what the first commandment is all about—a deep commitment of oneself to the God who has redeemed us. Thus preaching of the first commandment will seek to explore the nature of this love and its analogies on the human plane as a way into perceiving the depth of devotion to the Lord our God commanded in the first commandment.

The other dimension of the Shema that belongs to its preaching is the *totality* of this commitment, as reflected in the three phrases at the end: "with all your heart and with all your soul and with all your

---

4. On loving God, especially as characterized in Deuteronomy, see now Lapsley, "Feeling Our Way: Love."

might." The heaping up of these phrases and the threefold use of the word "all" signal the full and unstinting degree of love, commitment, and obedience. In Jewish and Christian tradition, the different phrases have served to emphasize the totality and also to point to the spheres of existence in which the commitment is manifest; for example, "with all your soul (*nephesh*)" equals the commitment of one's life even unto death, "with all your might" equals all that you have and own.[5]

Preaching the positive meaning of the first commandment will not confine itself to the Shema or its language. It will explore the nature and meaning of reverence and obedience, the fear of the Lord and what is meant by that notion. Especially central to the meaning of the first commandment is the matter of *trust*. When Martin Luther wrote his exposition of the first commandment in his Larger Catechism, this was the focus of attention:

> As I have often said, it is the trust and faith of the heart alone that make both God and an idol. If your faith and trust are right, then your God is the true one. Conversely, where your trust is false and wrong, there you do not have the true God.[6]

The critical issue of the commandment is the question wherein lies one's ultimate trust. It is the issue Jesus addresses in his words about serving God or Mammon. An exploration of that theme both in its development in Scripture and in its elaboration in relation to possible grounds of trust in human existence will help to open up the force and meaning of the first commandment.

3. Preach the first commandment out of the whole of the biblical story and out of texts that tell the story of the commandment. In other words, the whole of Scripture is before you on this theme. Indeed, one cannot really get at the force of the commandment without going into other texts. There are many stories of the first commandment, its obedience and its disobedience (more the latter than the former!), from the report of the making and worship of the golden calf in Exodus to the account of Shadrach, Meshach, and Abednego in the fiery furnace (Daniel 3). There is hardly any book of the Bible that does

5. On these phrases and the interpretation of the Shema in general, see especially McBride, "The Yoke of the Kingdom." Cf. Calvin, *The Sermons of John Calvin Upon the Fifth Book of Moses Called Deuteronomy*. For Calvin's comments on these phrases and for a more extensive treatment of the Shema, see Miller, *Deuteronomy*, 97–104.

6. Martin Luther, *The Large Catechism*, in *The Book of Concord*, 386.

not have something to say about how we live by this commandment. The Psalms are a rich resource, especially for interpreting the positive meaning of the commandment. For the matter of trust in God is central to the psalms of lament, thanksgiving, and trust. The image of God as refuge, expressed in various metaphors, is fundamental to the whole of the Psalter.[7]

The stories of the first commandment do not stop with Scripture. One will want to mine the history of both church and synagogue, from Cyprian and Rabbi Akiba to Dietrich Bonhoeffer and the Barmen Declaration of the Confessing Church, from the martyrs of the early church to the conscientious objectors of the American wars, to learn what it means to have "no other gods before me" and to love God with all that one is and all that one has.[8]

7. See in this regard, Creach, *Yahweh as Refuge.*

8. For a more extended discussion of the first commandment, see the author's *The God You Have.*

Sermons

On the Ministry

When Christ Calls

Old Testament Lesson: 1 Kings 19:15–21 (REB translation)
New Testament Lesson: Luke 9:51–62 (REB translation)

I HAVE A PROBLEM. I'm not sure that I have a sermon, but I know I have a problem. It is the two texts that have been read as Scripture. Not the two of them separately, but these two texts together. I did not put them together. I discovered them that way. Probably in a lectionary. But now that I have discovered them together I cannot pry them apart. And I don't know if I can live with them together. They create problems for me about Scripture, about discipleship, and about my family. And I think these two texts create the same problems for you, or I would not bother you with them this morning.

The Old Testament lesson tells of the call of Elisha, God's command to a burnt-out Elijah to go back into the heat of battle and take Elisha with him. Elijah is told by God to anoint new kings in Syria and Israel, both of whose present rulers are healthy and in powerful control. He is also told to anoint Elisha as his successor. The last comes first in the sequence of actions. Elijah runs into Elisha out plowing. It was either a Texas-sized ranch or Georgia hard red dirt because it took twelve teams of oxen to plough that field. Where I come from, you had to make do with one mule and a teenage boy. I assume Elisha was a little taken aback when this figure, Elijah, comes striding across the furrows and suddenly throws his coat over Elisha's shoulders and without a "Howdy do" or a "By your leave" turns around and walks on off. I'm impressed with Elisha, however, because he catches on to what this strange action was about even though Elijah didn't actually anoint him with oil. So Elisha figures it out quickly and immediately accepts the call: I will follow you (That's discipleship language, I trust you recognize. It is all over the Old Testament; we just don't notice it very much). But first, Elisha says "Let me go back and kiss Mom and Dad goodbye." He is aware of the significance of this call, that it means leaving home and family to go out and do dangerous deeds. Filial love and duty lead him to want to let his family know what is going on and be attentive to them. To which, Elijah, tersely replies, "Go ahead. I'm not doing anything to stop you."

So he goes back to his family, who after all, are about to lose not only a son but a good field hand. He throws a big goodbye barbecue, grilling his pair of oxen, partly because they make good barbecue, and partly to signal his change of vocation. He feeds "the people," that is, the kinfolk, and they all have a big farewell celebration. Then, according to the text, "he followed Elijah and became his disciple."

The New Testament lesson tells in more succinct but clearly pointed fashion of three encounters that Jesus has with persons who indicate a desire or willingness to follow him and become his disciples. The first volunteers. To which Jesus says, "Man, have you got any idea what you are getting into? Do you have any idea where I am headed? You can get up and come with me, but you won't ever sit down again, much less lie down for a quiet rest."

Then Jesus meets another person and tells him to come on and follow him. "Okay, but I have elderly parents that I can't just abandon. Let me get them in a good nursing home and I will be right with you." To which Jesus says, "Let them find their own nursing home or get the Welfare Department to help them. You have a job to do in the kingdom."

Finally he meets a third person who says, "All right, I will follow you, Lord; but first let me say goodbye to the folks back home." Sounds very much like Elisha. But Jesus gives a *very different* answer than did Elijah. It is a sharp rebuke in a saying that poses a clear either/or: No one who sets hand to the plow and then looks back is fit for the kingdom of God. You can't go home again, even to say goodbye to the folks.

And there, of course, is the rub and where these two texts strike sparks and create problems. One is a call to discipleship that seems to acknowledge and take account of human, and especially, family relationships as appropriate concerns even on the way of discipleship. The other is a radical call that allows no worry about personal concerns, no pause for filial duties, familial affections and responsibilities. A sharp conflict is created by these texts between the permission to go back and the demand to let everything go, between responsibility for life in this world and the relation-ships to which we are committed by birth or choice or circumstance and an unqualified commitment to the rule of God and service in the kingdom.

How do we decide between these two contradictory views? There is of course one obvious way of deciding, and it is characteristic of virtually all interpretation of the passage in Luke. If there is going to be a conflict be-tween Jesus and anyone else, even another text from the Bible, Jesus always wins. That is, Jesus here has set forth a more radical claim than Elijah, and that is the way of the kingdom. Seen this way the texts do not, therefore, exist in a real tension at all. Elijah has once more prepared the way for the coming of the anointed and now must step aside. In the encounter between Jesus and Torah, such a reading means that once more Torah has lost the battle, is set aside or superseded. The story told by the Old Testament and the obligations it has taught us to pay attention to as God's instructions for human life in community are no longer valid. There is a higher teaching, a more radical instruction. Honor of father and mother falls away before the command: Let the dead bury their own dead; go and announce the kingdom of God.

But the problem with that solution is that we only read the Torah and listen to its instruction because it is given to us by Christ as our Scriptures. And the issue I run up against as one who with others reads the Scriptures to listen for the word of God is not that we must respect the Torah because Jews respect it, and it is not a matter of figuring out the nuances of Paul's many words on the law to figure out what we now do with it. It is that you and I have read and continue to read the Torah under the inspiration of the Holy Spirit as the story of God's way that teaches something of our own way. And I cannot read the Scriptures schizophrenically: that is, pay attention to the Old Testament some of the time and set it aside some of the time. Obviously we have to deal with the multiplicity of voices in both the Old and New Testaments and the tensions often created by that fact. Yet Torah can never be an obstruction to hearing the word of Christ. And I cannot believe that Jesus ever meant that *his* words were to be an obstruc-tion to the hearing of the law and the prophets, not the one who said to the Sadducees that you know neither the Scriptures nor the power of God, not the one who quoted the Old Testament frequently and lived by it, who invoked the prophets in support of his own much criticized actions.

It is difficult, however, with these words of Jesus, because on more than one occasion Jesus talked of setting brother against sister and parent against child. And he talks as if that is his purpose. There is a radical claim here indeed, that one cannot just muddle through or slide by. In Luke, Jesus says "Whoever does not say goodbye to all he or she has cannot be a disciple of mine." And lest one miss the force of that demand, he frequently cites those things that matter most to us, our family and our possessions. Bonhoeffer put it in pithy terms: "Whenever Christ calls us, his call leads us to death."[1]

The word of our New Testament text, therefore, cannot be avoided. It is heard again and again from the lips of Jesus, who would put off those who lightly sign up for his cause and bids us sit down and tote up the cost before we enlist.

Does this mean that Elisha's request to honor father and mother is forever set aside for those who seek the kingdom and follow Christ? Is it that Jesus is finally once again the male voice who forces hierarchical choices upon us that rule out attention to that network of relationships in which life is lived? In one sense, yes, in that Jesus has taught us there *is one* hierarchy and only one that counts in the kingdom. It is the same one we learn from the Old Testament: "Hear O Israel, the LORD is our God, the LORD alone; and you shall love the LORD your God with all your heart, and with all your soul, and with all your might." Jesus's call to discipleship is a reminder that we are not finally just fellow travelers with him or cocreators with God. We are creatures, servants, disciples who are called to a love and obedience of God that directs our lives and transcends all other calls and loyalties. But it is both the Old Testament and Jesus who also have taught us that we live in relationships that matter and cannot be set lightly aside; it is Jesus who calls us not just servants but friends.

So I do not think we can simply choose one text over the other, or let one text supersede or cancel out the other. The texts remind us of *two different* things about our situation when Christ calls. One is the reminder we are given in Elisha's actions when called by God to a dangerous discipleship; that we live in a complex network of relationships that shape our life, matter to us, and for which we are responsible. When Christ calls, that does not mean a light and casual treatment of those human relationships that claim us—parent and child, wife and husband, friend and neighbor. In the service of Christ, I do not have to forget—I am not allowed to forget—that I am a husband, a father, a friend, a teacher. The second reminder from our text is that to live under God's rule and at the call of Christ is the *ultimate*

1. Bonhoeffer, *Discipleship*, 87.

claim within which all truly good, necessary, and penultimate claims are to be set. Those relationships that cannot be set aside lightly also cannot stand as barriers of resistance to doing God's will in the world, to living as citizens of a kingdom that is not the same as the present political order, to being members of a household and family that incorporates those nearest and dearest to us but only begins there.

I have no special wisdom about how to work out the tension created by these texts: the call of family alongside the call of Christ. I can think of two examples in which radical obedience and attention to family and friends were held together. These models may be more illuminating than any explanation. One is that of Jesus himself, who gave up everything for the sake of obedience to the will of God. In his last words and acts from the cross he looked at his mother who bore and loved him and at the disciple whom he loved, and he instructed them to care for one another. On the way to the Father, Jesus provided for his mother.

One of his later disciples, Dietrich Bonhoeffer, has reminded us more than most of the cost of discipleship to Jesus Christ. His most influential and widely read book is probably his *Letters and Papers from Prison*, written to friends and family in the months before his execution by the Gestapo. He shared with them the things that mattered most and showed his deep concern for their well-being. The only thing that disturbed him, he said in a letter to his parents, was that they would be worrying about him and thus losing sleep and not eating. At the close of the book, in one of his last letters, he wrote:

> Dear Mama,
>
> My New Year's wish for you and papa, and indeed for all of us,
> is that it may bring us at least an occasional glimpse of light,
> and that we may have the joy of reunion some day.
> May God keep you both well.
> With loving wishes, dear, dear, Mother, for a happy birthday.
> Your grateful son,
>
> Dietrich.[2]

I do not know well enough *how* one lives in the tension between the permission of Elijah and the no of Jesus; in hierarchy and network; under ultimate claim and in the midst of penultimate relationships that also matter. But the one word of this sermon is that this is where we are to live,

2. Bonhoeffer, *Letters and Papers*, 220.

in the midst of that tension, where father and mother, son and daughter, husband and wife, friends and neighbors really do matter in the dearest way; where those relationships are to be nurtured, cared for, borne and enjoyed, but also where God calls us to hold nothing so dear that it cannot be relinquished for the sake of the kingdom of peace and justice. This is where discipleship is not an abstract concept but a walk in the world along the dangerous track that Jesus carved out for us, the way of the kingdom.

There may, in fact, be living space in that tension. Perhaps in living we shall find that in those varying connections of love and friendship we discover something of what it means to love God. And in loving God we may learn not to reject the devoted love of those most dear but how it is we truly love and are loved.

That is what this communion table is about. It is a gathering of family and friends, which is where God has set our lives. So love and care. It is also a revelation of the costly way of Christ, which is where God has set our feet. So go and risk.

What You Need to Know

Scripture Lesson: Matthew 22:23–33

I AM SPEAKING OVER the heads of the faculty this afternoon—at least, in one sense. What I mean is that this sermon is directed specifically to those of you who are about to graduate: our friends, former students, and future colleagues in the ministry. The rest of you are welcome to listen in to see if there is something appropriate to your own life and work.

The title I have given the sermon is somewhat audacious, as I am well aware. It is presumptuous of me at this last moment to claim to be able to tell you what you need to know as you go forth into the ministry of Christ. But I take the answer to the implicit questions in the sermon title, "What do you need to know?" from our Lord. It is not my own. I am a tradent, passing on the word, and suggesting its appropriateness for those who leave this school to enter into the service of that same Lord. And what I have to say will be brief, as Jesus's own words were brief. This text is no ten-page list of competencies for the ministry.

Jesus's response to the Sadducees who question him is an ad hoc word on which I am now generalizing. It is a controversy pericope that I am turning into a piece of instruction for disciples. It is a *particular* word to a *particular* question, and I am suggesting it is the *continuing* word for *all questions*. So one risks transforming what is a limited saying of Jesus into a much broader word, a rebuke into a word of instruction and comfort. But I think I can get away with that on two grounds.

1. There is some sense in which the Scriptures regard no words of Jesus as casual. A kind of oft-ridiculed reflection of that conviction is found in those red-letter Bible versions that highlight all of Jesus's words in red type. I suppose that would be the case even if he only said *kai ho*, "and the" one time. And President Gillespie would probably be able to preach a sermon on even that Jesus saying! So also the often-ridiculed

71

project of a number of New Testament scholars getting together to decide and let the world know which of the sayings are really Jesus's words suggests that these particular words have a broader significance.

2.   But I can draw upon this text of conflict between Jesus and a Jewish party, the Sadducees, as a word to you about your ministry in this time and place also because what Jesus accuses the Sadducees of needing to know and of not knowing, in their confrontation with him, are two things that dominate Jesus's own ministry from beginning to end. The Scriptures and the power of God are always present and out front in Jesus's ministry, in what he says and does. At the critical beginning of his ministry, in Luke's account, it is the Scriptures that Jesus opens to explain what he is about, why God has sent him. And what they point to is the power of God at work in this one in our midst, a power for healing and release, for seeing and for breaking the bonds that enchain us (Luke 4:16–21).

That, of course, is what *you* need to know every bit as much as the Sadducees—two things: the Scriptures and the power of God. Because they did not really know either one, they sought to destroy him. Your ignorance of those things cannot destroy the Lord you serve, only betray him.

I do not really know how one can ever measure success in the ministry, or whether we should even try. If so, such measurement generally has to be done by others than by ourselves. The issue that those engaged in ministry have to raise about themselves is that of faithfulness. I want to suggest to you that among those things without which faithful ministry is difficult or impossible, knowledge of the Scriptures and knowledge of the power of God are at the top.

In urging the knowledge of the Scriptures as essential to a faithful ministry, I risk reminding you of the obvious, but it cannot be said too loudly. Nor do I think that the people in whose midst you will carry out your ministry will disagree with this commendation of the knowledge of the Scriptures as a first order of business. The study of the Bible is something that has consumed much of your energies during your years here. And part of why I am setting that before you once again is because the knowledge of the Scriptures is not a hoop to be jumped through as a part of theological education. I assure you the Sadducees were at the top of their seminary classes. The knowledge of the Scriptures is the lifeblood of your ministry. But it is only at a beginning. The learning of the Scriptures is a task to which each of us is to give our continuing efforts so that they become a part of who we are and the source of our ministry in both word and deed. I trust that I will not be misunderstood as one member of a department of the seminary engaging in special pleading in behalf of the primacy of his field. Not at all. I don't know whether Jesus would have been caught dead on a theological faculty, but I doubt if it would have been in the Bible Department in any event. Indeed it is my judgment that in the work of the ministry you are fundamentally theologians and pastors, not biblical scholars. But the source and ground of that theological and pastoral work is always the Word of God.

The knowledge of the Scriptures belongs to the church's ministry for two purposes: *to draw from it in every endeavor and to be shaped by it in your whole being*. This means, at least, that one is to become so at home in the whole of Scripture, to learn to walk around in it as familiar territory, that one draws instinctively from it and turns always to it in preaching and teaching; in the struggle with the difficult moral issues that will arise in the congregation or the social context in which you live and work; in the range of your pastoral care, whether it is in formal counsel to troubled persons, the ministry to the sick and dying, or that less defined sustaining of the souls of your people in their daily endeavors to live the Christian life amidst perplexity, anxiety, guilt, fear, and doubt of self and God. In such situations, your people will want in some fashion, often ill-defined if not unrealized, to hear, as we have put it more often in the past, a word from the Lord. The words that you have from the Lord are to be found where they have always been found, there in the Scriptures.

When I was ordained and installed as a pastor of a congregation, my father said these words to me. I pass them on to you:

> Open the Book with but one prayerful and passionate desire: to let it speak through you God's word to his people. The Bible is your book; see that nothing less is offered to your hearers. Bring only *beaten oil* to the Temple—no other offering is worthy of the one who called you or sufficient to human needs. Place prayer and study of the Word *early* in every day and let nothing interfere with this. The most worn rug in this church should be the one under your study desk.

That other thing you need to know, if I overhear Jesus's conversation with the Sadducees correctly, is simply and impressively *the power of God*. For the minister of Christ, to know the power of God as a reality that has shaped her past and the history of that community of which she or he is a part and also to expect with confidence that God's power is at work *now* in the midst of this congregation and *this* people and in and through one's own ministry is as fundamental as all of the knowledge and skill that those of us in theological education can teach.

The danger of such a word, of course, is that it can be misconstrued by pastor or congregation as permission for laziness and naiveté, for the pastoral and theological error of thinking that divine power is something easily at hand, like chips to be cashed in—a danger that is present all over the place, if the TV evangelists are any indicator. The power of God is mysterious and wonderful. The Spirit blows where it will. And the work of God is not apart from *human* work in the *service* of God. But when all of that is said and done, the faithfulness of the ministry includes not only that disciplined hard work that is inescapable and properly required of us but also a trust that God is truly at work in the life of your people and will empower both their work and your own.

We tend too easily not to expect very much, and so we pray too little and despair too quickly. Like Israel in the wilderness, we see all the great and tall and fortified cities before us and forget the power of God that has given victory and nurtured and provided. The transforming power of God to heal broken bodies and minds, to soften hard hearts, to teach the ways of justice and peace, is promised to us and can be counted upon. But the Deuteronomic story suggests that God's power needs to be seen and trusted and known, else we will not know how to operate when we cross over the boundary, into that new time and space that God has given to us. The weakness to which Israel's story alerts us is not finally a matter of incompetence or lack of gifts or even laziness. It is a weakness of the spirit whose mind is not stayed on God and whose expectations for what the Lord can do in the midst of God's people are too timid. When in the church's liturgy you declare God's forgiveness, when you pray at beds of pain for God's strength and comfort, do so in the full knowledge that God's wonders never cease, that resurrection—life out of death—is not a concept. That is God's thing!

The rural priest in George Bernanos's famed novel *The Diary of a Country Priest* lacked many of the personal gifts that one would want in a pastor and was not well trained for the priesthood. He performed ineptly much of the time. But he knew, as he said with his last breath, that "Grace is everywhere." Take that conviction with you into your ministry. It is a reminder of whose power is ultimately at work. Believing it, you can, like Paul, do all things through Christ, who will give you strength.

The Prophet's Sons and Daughters

Old Testament Lesson: Amos 7:10–17

New Testament Lesson: Acts 3:17–26

BACCALAUREATES ARE A ROUTINE that goes with commencement. For this community, however, baccalaureates can never be routine, even when they are not on Friday afternoon. On the way to commencement, those who are called to Christ's service gather first in his praise. The subject matter of our proclamation is given to us by the occasion itself. It is the ministry. The successful completion of your preparation for service in the ministry of the gospel—remember that is what this is about, not just getting a degree—and the involvement of all the rest of us—family, friends, and teachers—in that enterprise is what brings us together.

Of all the many things appropriate to say on such occasion, I want to make one proposal. It is simply that as ministers of the gospel you are the sons and daughters of the prophets and so invested with and encumbered with *a prophetic ministry*. I would like to think a little bit about what that means in the light of Scripture and with particular reference to two things: the *conditions* of a prophetic ministry and the *task* of a prophetic ministry.

THE CONDITIONS OF A PROPHETIC MINISTRY

The stories of the prophets are fairly clear about what is the primary condition for the prophetic work. It is a *sense of being called* and of living and *working under authority*. Those are, of course, one and the same thing. The call is of God and the authority of the prophet is tied to that call. He or she stands under the constraint of God and as bearer of God's word. Amos and his fellow prophets did not assume their functions in God's governance and purpose out of a desire or a disposition or a particular bent for that sort of thing. Oh, some may have done that, but they are not the ones to whom we still listen. Quite the contrary, you will recall that most of those prophets whose words still address us objected to the very idea—as well they might.

In some cases, as for example, that of Jeremiah, the call is expressed in a kind of election that belongs to his very being: "Before I formed you in the womb I knew you, and before you were born I consecrated you" (Jer 1:5). His calling is not a happenstance. It is what he was born to be and to do by the very plan and intention of God. If Reformed Christians, and I trust many others also, say with vigor and joy that we know ourselves, even before we were born, to have been elected in love, Jeremiah's call lets us know that there were and are some who discover that they were, even before they were born, elected into vocation, into a prophetic ministry.

There is nothing accidental about God's call, though it may be experienced "by accident," so to speak. I am sure it was a big surprise to Jeremiah. And Amos lets us know that he had a very good vocation as a business man before, in his words, "and the LORD took me from following after the flock and said, 'Go prophesy to my people.'"

Participation in the ministry is not primarily a job or a contract. It is not something we are hired or even invited to do. However it may be experienced, the ministry is something into which we are called. We come to that conviction in various ways, some of them more like an actual calling, a conscious sense of being impelled into the ministry from beyond oneself, others more like a discernment that is rooted in one's self-assessment and self-understanding, one's openness to the world and to the gospel. However, that conviction may come, the ministry is created by the call of God, and the authority under which you preach and teach is inherent in that calling, in your self-understanding as one who is under God's constraint and God's demand and whose word is the word of the Lord.

That calling, however, is to a task. And for the prophetic ministry that means more to a task than to an office. Amos may have been a business man, but he is now a prophet. The big deal, however, is not being a prophet, assuming a role. In fact, what Amos says to the Dean of the National Cathedral at Bethel is not that "I am a prophet," but rather "the LORD took me and said, 'Go prophesy to my people Israel'" (Amos 7:15). And Isaiah hears the words, "Whom shall I send and who will go for us?" (Isa 6:8). And to Jeremiah comes the word of the Lord: "You shall go to all to whom I send you, and you shall speak whatever I command you . . ." (Jer 1:7). The prophetic ministry is the service of God *under assignment*. One may indeed speak of the prophet's mantle, of the descent of the spirit, of an anointing, all ways of saying one now belongs to this category or this group or office in God's kingdom. An identity is thereby given. But the identity is *missional*. What is most prominent is the sense of being commanded and sent and commissioned to do something.

So what is that task? If we read through the prophets, we might list a whole bunch of things. Let me suggest that underneath their many oracles and many situations are three things that belong to any prophetic ministry:

1. In a prosperous, self-satisfied, and self-authenticating society, the prophets and their sons and daughters bring the power of God's word in criticism of all forms of self-interest that neglect the weak and the small and the powerless and do not set righteousness and justice as the primary criteria for deciding what to do and for whom to speak. The divine insistence on justice in the human community brooks no qualifications. Psalm 82 reminds us that gods cannot stay gods without providing justice for the weak. And the faithful prophets and their sons and daughters remind the people of God that they cannot be God's people and be indifferent to the distortions of human life and human society that wreak havoc with fairness and justice, with what it takes to make and to keep human life human.

From Amos and his prophetic sisters and brothers we learn what we cannot ignore in our own time and our own prophetic ministry, and that is the centrality of the *legal* and *economic* systems for the maintenance of justice. The prophetic critique carries in it a clear understanding of what it is that God seeks in the human community. The notion of justice inherent in the message of the prophets has been accurately described in this way:

> All citizens should have a share in the control of the society's basic economic good as the instrument of their status, access to rights, and freedom. The administration of order should protect and support this distribution against economic and political processes that erode it. Institutional law should be subject to interpretation and correction by the worth of persons and moral values. Wealth which prejudices the welfare and rights of others is unjust. Treatment of the least favored in the society is the fundamental criterion of the achievement of justice.[3]

3. Mays, "Justice," 16.

In the face of a human society where such a notion of God's justice was ignored or trampled underfoot—and stronger language than that is often used—the prophets did four things:

a.   they announced God's judgment on a society that could not live by righteousness and justice and trust in the Lord alone;

b.   they sought repentance and a mending of the ways: "Amend your ways and doings," preached Jeremiah in the temple (Jer 7:3);

c.   they appealed to the *faith* and *conscience* of their people in simple but clear ways, calling on them to hate evil and love good, to render in their courts judgments that are true and make for peace; and

d.   they confronted the powers that be, whether by intention or by outcome, and called for a change of direction under threat of God's judgment.

In such a prophetic ministry as that suggests, it does not matter where your pulpit is or who is your audience. Where God's righteousness and justice are not in practice, there the sons and daughters of the prophets name the sin and call for another way of doing things. That may be in the pulpit on a Sunday morning. It may be in conversation with officers of the church. It may be in the classroom. It may be in letters to the newspaper, addresses to civic clubs, or on the streets— wherever. The niceties and distinctions that we sometimes worry over between civil religion and ecclesiastical context, between church and state, preaching and meddling, were not and are not of consequence for the prophetic ministry. It is not something that operates here and there, a couple of days a week. It goes on constantly in public and in private, in preaching and pastoral care. To Ezekiel God said, "I have made you a sentinel for the house of Israel; whenever you hear a word from my mouth, you shall give them a warning from me" (Ezek 3:17). That is a *pastoral* task, to be *God's sentry* in the midst of your people, alerting them, together and individually, when the word of God is not present in the life of the community and when God's justice is not the order of the day.

2.   The second aspect of a prophetic ministry is this: In whatever the situation, the sons and daughters of the prophets are charged with imagining a different way, with envisioning and announcing the new

possibility of God's way in the world, what Walter Brueggemann calls an alternative community, and what Scripture means when it talks about a covenant people and the kingdom of God, a community of people in time and space who live by the rule of God and by God's ways, where the care of the weakest is the criterion of a just society, where one's ultimate trust is not in the gods of productivity or in Wall Street, or even in an Alan Greenspan, all of them weak reeds, but in the Lord of all the worlds that are, the creator of the universe, from whom cometh every good and perfect gift.

Such a community is found here and there in congregation after congregation. The prophetic task is to be the bearer of God's word to effect and mobilize that community of faithful obedience. If the Scriptures are the plumb line by which the prophets' sons and daughters measure the faithfulness of the contemporary church and call it to account, they are also the impetus for imagining a truly peaceable kingdom, for envisioning a city of righteousness, whose builder and maker is God, where old people can sit in safety in the parks and children play in the streets, where nations come together to study peace and not to build new armaments and missile shields, where the nations pour their resources into economic production for the common good and the enhancement of life for all. The prophet's sons and daughters dare to proclaim what is impossible in a world that lives by the pragmatic and reasonable because they *know* the answer to the question: "Is anything too difficult for the LORD?" (Gen 18:14) and are willing to hang their hats on that conviction, maybe even give their lives for it.

3. Where they find themselves in the midst of a defeated, undone, and despairing community, the sons and daughters of the prophets dare *to announce the good news of God's power and God's presence*. There is a difference between cheap grace and the power of the gospel. I cannot tell you what it is. You have to find it out in the midst of your people, whoever and wherever they are. When you do, then, like the prophets of Israel and like John the Baptist's gnarled finger in Mathias Grünewald's great painting of the crucifixion at Isenheim, you will find yourselves pointing always to the one in whose ministry you are about to enter, whose presence sustains in every circumstance, whose help is truly sufficient for every pain.

What then about possible outcomes for such a prophetic ministry? I can think of a couple. One is burnout. That clearly happened to the prophets; read your Bible. Elijah took off and left town in utter discouragement and fear. And Jeremiah complained all the time and was ready to give it all up. As best I can tell, however, burnout was not allowed for the prophets, and it may not be allowed for their sons and daughters. Elijah heard a voice saying: "What are you doing here?" (1 Kgs 19:9) and was sent back to confront the royal powers, an even more radical task. Jeremiah was told, "If you are having difficulty with a congregation like this one, what are you going to do with the hornets' nest that is just in front of you. You think the Boston Marathon was hard, what are you going to do when I put you in the Kentucky Derby—on foot!"

But there is no demitting the task, no words—"Lord, I didn't bargain for this when I answered your call"—that will get you out of the prophetic ministry. I wish I could give you an easier word than that, but it would not be what the Bible says. But maybe, just maybe there can be other outcomes: What about a congregation renewed and committed to God's way, to the proclamation of the good news in every nook and cranny of our society and our world? What about the kingdom coming to life in the midst of a people pledged to God's way of righteousness and mercy and trust? What about students who hear your words and find their consciences forever disturbed? I don't know. Is anything too difficult for God?

And what about fringe benefits for the prophets' sons and daughters? Well, I *can* tell you about that. There aren't any. You will have to find the goodies elsewhere. I wish I could tell you that I thought Amos felt satisfied at the end of the day or that Isaiah went home to play catch with little Shear-yashub with a sense of a job well-done. He probably went home worried about what he was going to have to do the next day that would make his people even more resistant to the divine word.

No, there are no fringe benefits to the prophetic ministry—except one: the promise of God's companioning presence along the way. And you should realize the reason for such a promise is that you are going to need it. But when you do, you will have it. The promise of Immanuel is specifically a word to the prophets: "I am with you." In the fiery trials, in the heat of the battle, in the lassitude of indifference, in the face of resistance to the word of the Lord, in the times when it all falls apart and your very well-being and maybe even that of your family is threatened, "I am with you." If you think that means everything will work out all right, I'm not sure. I just know that the grace of the Lord Jesus Christ and the love of God and the fellowship of the Holy Spirit will indeed be with you. That grace and love will have to be sufficient. I believe it will.

Stewards of the Mysteries of God

Old Testament Lesson: Deuteronomy 4:32–40
New Testament Lesson: 1 Corinthians 4:1–5

IEXPECT THAT THE mental state of most of you within twenty-four hours of receiving your diploma is pretty much, "Let's get out of here." That is understandable. You have been at it hard, in most cases for three or more years. The time may have gone quickly, but it is by definition preparatory for something else, and now it is time to move on to the something else. (I realize that for some of you that may be more study!). Before you do move on, however, we set this time apart to close off your years here as they began, in the worship of God, an enacted, public, visible reminder of who we are and what we are about. We also set it apart as a time for some reflection in the moment of transition, thinking together about where you have been and where you are going.

While there are many ways to go about that, it has seemed to me appropriate to turn our attention to one of those moments of self-reflection on his ministry that Paul occasionally lets seep out of his message to the churches who were his ministerial field. In this case, it is a few verses of chapter 4 of his first letter to the church at Corinth, a pretty ragged congregation that seems to have been giving him a hard time. They were apparently rating him negatively against better preachers and in general scrutinizing his ministry and griping about it while holding themselves in very high esteem.

That may not sound like a very promising place to go to inspire persons on the verge of going into the ministry. But that, my friends, is where you may find yourself at some point. And like Paul, you may realize that it is in just such spotlighted moments of outside scrutiny that you will want to check yourself on what you are about and so discover whose judgment really matters.

Paul begins where he must begin and where he always begins, setting forth a definition of himself and those like him—"think of us"—as "servants of Christ." I am passing that on from Paul with the suggestion that you make it your primary self-understanding as you take up the calling of the Christian ministry. You leave here and go out, whatever the particular call may be, as servants of Christ. You do not go primarily to be a pastor or to teach or to build up the church or to mend broken souls. One's understanding of the ministry may involve all sorts of things that are tied to particular ministries or tasks, to certain competencies or affinities—I am a teaching minister; you may be a minister to the poor or to young people. But these are not the heart of the matter, not the orienting center. You go as servants of Christ, those whose competence and ineptness, whose pastoral counseling and preaching, are features of an existence primarily defined by the fact that we are servants of a Lord. All we do is shaped by that point of reference.

We should note that Paul's term for "servants" here is not quite what we might expect. It is not the familiar *doulos* or *diakonos*, the standard New Testament terms for "slave" or "servant." It is *hypēretēs*, a word that indeed means "the service of another" but puts the focus less on the activity of service than it does on the free choice to follow direction. It could refer to various kinds of assistants, helpers, persons who worked under the direction and control of another: a physician's assistant, a synagogue attendant, a priest's helper; as one person has defined the term, "one who assists another as the instrument of his will."[1] Paul never uses the term again, but he had heard it at a crucial point in his life. When on the Damascus road, on his way under the authority of the chief priests to persecute the Christians, he was stopped by a blinding light from heaven and a voice that spoke to him and forever changed his life. The words that voice spoke were, "Stand on your feet, for I have appeared to you for this purpose, to appoint you a servant (*hypēretēn*)" (Acts 26:16).

As with Paul, what shapes our ministry is the awareness and conviction that we are *under orders*, that like the pointing finger of John the Baptist in Matthias Grünewald's great painting of the crucifixion, all our gestures in preaching, all our offered hands in ministry, all our arms lifted in prayer, point in one direction, to the one who has called us into his service and under whose orders we go forth into the world. Like the *hypēretēs* in the synagogue at Nazareth in Luke 4, when Christ reads the Scriptures,

1. Rengstorff, "*hypēretēs*," 539.

you hold the book—and hold it well—that's what all this exegetical and theological and homiletical work has been about. Like the *hypēretēs* of the word who delivered the tradition about Jesus Christ to Luke, so you are under the direction of that word to pass on the tradition about the Lord. Think of us as servants of Christ, those who are under orders from their Lord and directed by his word.

But that is not all Paul offers us by way of self-definition. He thinks of himself and bids us think of ourselves as "stewards of God's mysteries." And each of those words is an important part of his claim and your calling. It is *God's* mysteries that are entrusted to us, says Paul. Never forget that. We sometimes speak of the pastor as the theologian of the community. That sounds very much like how an academic community would regard the work of the ministry. If so, then *mea culpa*. I think that is *exactly* what Paul is talking about, the conviction that his whole life was set to speak about God and what God was doing in Jesus Christ and what that had to do with everything, from the way masters and slaves related to each other to how you ate food, to your attitude to the state, and how you spoke to your elders and officers.

There are many things you will do in your ministry, but all of them are tied to your commitment to the things of God, to the speaking and preaching and acting that point to the one who has made us, in whose hands our lives are cared for, and who calls us to the life that does not end. In those moments that mark human life in regular fashion—birth, baptism, marriage, children, and all the daily provision of life that each of us receives, you will help your people, your students, your families, your rich and your poor, find and discern the work of God. In those moments that sting and cripple and sadden and destroy our lives, you will bring the strong comfort of God. You will point to a source of strength that is there when all human strength has finally fallen into nothingness.

But what does Paul mean when he says that it is the *mysteries* of God that are entrusted to our care? For Paul and for us, the mystery of God is most clearly revealed in the gospel, in that good news that overcomes all the bad news that can ever come down our path. It is a mystery that the wise cannot discern, only a fool for Christ. To be a steward of the mysteries of God is to be entrusted with the gospel, to be now and forever the bearer of a piece of good news to those you serve: You don't have to be afraid. I am with you. I will deliver you. That is the good news underlying everything else, the word from the Lord that can transform the lives of your people. Do not hold it back, you who are becoming stewards of the mysteries of God.

Paul is quite clear what it means to be *stewards* of the divine mysteries: "Moreover," he writes, "it is required of stewards that they be found trustworthy." And I am going to risk the claim that that is what you have been about over these past years here at Princeton Seminary, to prepare yourselves to be stewards of the mysteries of God, but more specifically so that you may be found trustworthy in that enterprise. You are going to be responsible for some pretty powerful stuff. Every time you walk into a pulpit, your stewardship of those mysteries is on the line. Every time you stand by a sick bed of any sort, you are responsible for the secrets of God. When you lay your hands on the head of a child in baptism and say "I baptize you in the name of the Father, and of the Son, and of the Holy Spirit," you are a steward of God's mysteries. When you stand over the grave of a parishioner and say "I am the resurrection and the life" and speak to the ones whose loss is beyond bearing, you are at that moment entrusted with the mysteries of God. When you say to the congregation those amazing words, "I declare unto you in the name of Jesus Christ, your sins are forgiven," you are steward of the mysteries of God.

This is not something confined to ministerial acts as pastor and preacher or to ordination as such. So those of you whose vocation in service to Christ carries you into teaching and healing ministries, do not think you can avoid the power that is in your hands and the mystery that is given to you. As you learn to teach, learn that what you are doing is a holy act. When you take up the things of God, whether they are biblical texts, theological doctrines, or acts of ministry—when you take them up in order to teach others, know that you are dealing always with what is holy and with the mysteries of God.

What is required in all this, Paul tells us, is that we be trustworthy. The issue of the ministry is not finally success. It is faithfulness. It is the refusal to forsake the gospel in a world that does not believe there really is good news or to tell lies in a world that seeks easy answers to the deepest questions. I really do believe the ministry is a very precious calling. How precious it is you will come to know as you experience the power of the ministry to heal souls, to change lives, to make the wounded whole, through God's power at work within you to shape and mold minds and hearts to the faithful service of God.

Three weeks after I arrived to begin my ministry in a small South Carolina church, straight out of school and not even ordained yet, our Sunday lunch in the manse next door to the church was interrupted by a woman running down the driveway shouting, "The McDowells have been in a terrible car accident on the way home from church." I hardly knew who the McDowells were. I did know Lester was chair of the Board of Deacons and Jane a member of the choir. Even worse, I did not know what to do. The only thing I could think of was to go to the one hospital in town. So I did, and shortly after I arrived the family was brought in on stretchers in various kinds of terrible condition. Lester's father John McDowell, a former clerk of session who had dropped out of church with alcohol problems and whom I had not even met, showed up about the same time. I introduced myself to him and in his shock and grief he looked at me with astonishment and said "When did you get here?" He could not believe that I was there before any of the victims arrived. I, of course, was there because I did not know anywhere else to go. But that one act was a transforming moment and opened the doors to a caring ministry with that family that has not ended yet, though Lester died that afternoon and his wife Jane has been in a wheelchair able to speak only with difficulty for over forty years. My friends, there is nothing else you can ever do that can give so much with so little and receive so much for so little.

The faithful preaching of the gospel in the world in which we live, however, does not always heal the wounds. Sometimes it uncovers festering sores; sometimes it identifies with terrible clarity the sin that the Lord alone can overcome. You are playing with fire when you seek to speak and interpret the word of God. That is a dangerous occupation. One can get burned. And the greatest risk to your health and well-being may be the God whose mysteries have been entrusted to you. The one who is not seen or comprehended, who comes to us in the fire that illuminates but cannot be touched or grasped. This is no game we are playing. It is the responsibility to think and speak and act about what matters most in this world, to seek to interpret to human beings their whence and whither, to dare to help people encounter the one who made them and this universe, to offer the word of life that we have no power to give except as we are under orders.

So what's the bottom line? Paul knew, and we probably should pay attention. He says, "It really matters very little to me if I should be judged/ scrutinized by you or by any human court." I doubt that means Paul was invulnerable to the criticisms of his peers and colleagues in the ministry or those of his congregations at Corinth and elsewhere. He was quite human and spoke of those things that did him in or moved him to tears. And yet he says, "it matters very little." I believe you can say the same thing—but only because of what Paul goes on to say: "It is *the Lord* who judges me" (1 Cor 4:4).

It is not my colleagues or your teachers, who have given you lots of grades, not your future elders or bishops, who will scrutinize your work very carefully. It is not finally whether a congregation thinks you have blown it or are the best minister they have ever had. "It is the Lord who judges me," says Paul—and you also. I hope you find that word both encouraging and scary—because it really is.

The calling is worth the risk, my friends and fellow servants of Christ. To be under orders to this Lord means to be free from all other powers. To be entrusted with the mysteries of this God is to have in your hands that which is more precious than anything else there is. So go, and be faithful with what is being entrusted to you. And may the one who has called you bless you in all that you do.

By What Authority?

Old Testament Lesson: Jeremiah 23:16–22
New Testament Lesson: Luke 20:1–8

THE OCCASION THAT BRINGS me into your pulpit this morning is the installation of your pastor. It is appropriate that the occasion be one in which we think together about the ministry. I do not, however, want to do that in the abstract but rather in the context of our attending to the words of Scripture and the ways it illumines our understanding of what we are about and, even more important, what God is about in our midst. In this instance, the text that is the basis for our thinking together is Luke's report of an encounter between Jesus and the various religious leaders of Jerusalem and particularly the question they put to him: "Tell us, by what authority you are doing these things?" The question was confrontive then, and it is confrontive now. It cuts to the heart of things and so forces out all other matters.

By what authority? The word *authority* implies all the freight that weighty term carries: right, power, source. It is a term that modern culture tends to view with a high degree of suspicion, either because it assumes an infringement upon our freedom to do and say and believe whatever we wish, or because we easily transpose the term *authority* into *authoritarian*. The latter is a mode of living and acting that expects or offers absolute and unthinking obedience, where freedom to decide and act are no longer operative.

But *authority*, and more specifically the authority of Jesus and those who act in his behalf, is an issue that pervades the Gospels. One cannot escape it. There is no doubt that both John and Jesus speak and act with authority. That is a conclusion drawn by the crowds who hear them. It is spread abroad and becomes the basis of Jesus's fame: "They were astounded at his teaching, for he taught them as one having authority . . . What is this? A new teaching—with authority!" (Mark 1:22, 27). And whenever the religious leaders ask Jesus: Why do you do this? Why do your disciples do that? those are always questions about Jesus's authority. Finally, near the end, just after Jesus's cleansing of the temple (Luke 19:45–48), they now put the question very bluntly: "By what authority do you do these things?" The issue of Jesus's authority comes to a climax precisely in this encounter.

I want to suggest that the question so posed tells us some important things about Jesus, who he was and what he was about. But it also has a continuing reverberation in its implicit address to those who speak in Jesus' name: By what authority do you do these things? It is about Jesus and it is about us.

The question then was a direct challenge to Jesus by the chief priests, the scribes, and the elders. You know who those people were. They were the leading ministers (the priests), the scribes; that is, the legal or theological experts who later are described as those who like to walk around in long robes and love to be greeted with respect (sort of like theological professors, don't you think?); and the elders, the leading laymen of Jerusalem (no women, of course, at that point). I take it that means Jesus had the whole presbytery after him, though they called it the council there, and eventually, of course, as we are told by Luke in the preceding chapter, they want to kill him.

We should take note of the context in which the challenge is made. We are given two clues about that. One is in the possible reference or meaning of "these things." "By what authority are you doing *these things*?" The leaders may well have had in mind Jesus's cleansing of the temple—an event, described in the immediately preceding verses—that aroused the anger of the religious authorities and became the last straw in their conflict with him.

We are told also that this question about Jesus's authority came "as he was teaching the people in the temple and telling the good news." The authority that Jesus manifests is most evident in the acts of teaching and preaching the gospel. It is there also in acts of healing and forgiveness, but where Jesus gets confronted and challenged is precisely at the point of the evident power of the gospel: the good news that in Jesus the kingdom of God is at hand, that in Jesus God is with us, that in him we can find forgiveness. In one sense, the powers that be were right to raise the question. The claims implicit in the teaching and preaching of Jesus are immense. The gospel of God breaks open here in the claim that the kingdom is at hand, not because anything has changed politically, then or now, but because God has sent this one powerfully into our midst.

The issue implicit in Jesus's preaching the gospel has been described by the theologian James Mays in this way:

It is "whether you find his life so convincing that you turn in faith constantly to his presence in the gospel and decide to give your living over to the program and policy and power of the government he represents and presents in his life." The question then, Mays suggests, is:

> Is his presence in the gospel reality enough to be the basis of credibility and the reason of hope for you? Does he give you your way of viewing life and history?
>
> Or is he some sort of peripheral assumption in the congregation, a kind of trademark to which we have become accustomed?
>
> Then our consciousness, our world-view—our faith—have nothing to do with him. For whatever else he is, Jesus of Nazareth is no trademark for what already is, nor will he settle easily into the commonplace of our life. He, the foe of the devil, this warrior with the demonic, this toucher of lepers, this true sword of flesh against hypocrisy, compassion's challenge to every status quo, giver of bread, stiller of storms, lover of the crippled and the weak and the little, enactor of the passion for God, who though he were dead yet lives and lives because he died on the cross; . . . he can be no commonplace.[1]

The good news was there in who he was, what he did, and what he said. And in the face of that, the powers that be found their own authority and control cut out from under them. So they challenged him precisely at the critical point. If his authority was only a human claim and not from God, then they had him. There is no human power, no human authority that can offer such radical good news and make such claims about our life and world and what God is doing in it.

So the religious leaders put the question of Jesus's authority to him and he answered them. Or did he? That is a matter of debate. Certainly he gave them no straight answer. Instead, he asked them a question: "Did the baptism of John come from heaven, or was it of human origin?" Some see in Jesus's response a sign of his cleverness and a refusal to answer the challenge. Instead he traps them in their own trap, knowing that whichever way they answer, they are caught. But I think this is not merely the device of a clever teacher, though Jesus was surely that. Jesus's question back to

1. Mays, "Jesus Came Preaching," 38–39.

them is not a dodge, however. Rather it forces his hearers and challengers to remember the message of John and indeed to remember Jesus's own baptism by John confirmed by the word from above, "This is my beloved Son." The question about John that Jesus puts to the religious leaders is the same one they have asked him. In dealing with *his* question, they will deal with their own.

Even more important, however, is that the meaning of Jesus's presence and work is not a matter of a simple answer to the question, "By what authority?" The simple answer "My authority is from God" allows for theological challenge and possible dismissal. Instead, the question that comes back from Jesus places the hearers, then and now, once again before the personal decision about what we do make of this Christ. So it is that our questions about the Christ, like those of the priests and scribes, regularly are turned back upon us. They become questions to us with which we are going to have to deal. They do not receive quick and simple answers. They do not even receive answers. We are instead confronted with the reality of Jesus and his teaching and preaching, and we have to decide in light of that, in response to the gospel, not because someone has told us this one is God. Here is the good news. What will you do?

But, remember, today we are going to install one of Christ's ministers. So where does she come in? It is not a whole lot different from where all of us come in. There is a further dimension, however, to this text. For the issue of authority is present not only in the teaching and preaching of Jesus, and the implications of the text are not only about Jesus and the good news he preached. The Gospel stories tell us that he also *gave his disciples authority,* over demons and to cure diseases, and sent them out to proclaim the kingdom of God and to heal. He also warned them they might not be welcome when they did this and might have to get out of town quickly (Luke 9:1–6).

The question "by what authority?" confronts every minister of the gospel, every time he or she teaches and preaches, in all acts of healing and forgiveness. To each of us it is incumbent to know both the source of our authority and that the question about our authority will confront us in various ways. It would be easy to say that the source of the minister's authority is the same source as Jesus's authority: the God who sent him and who sends us. But that answer, even if correct, was too simple then, and it is too simple now. By what authority will be evident in the faithfulness of the ministry, in the word rightly preached and only after careful listening to what the Scriptures say. By what authority will be demonstrated in the care and cure of souls by those who know there is a balm in Gilead and are unafraid to offer it in the name of Jesus Christ. By what authority will be manifest in the correspondence of deeds and words, of a life that is itself a manifestation of the gospel, of God's good news of forgiveness and grace.

Even when all that happens, the minister of the gospel will be faced with the same paradox that confronted her Lord. She will find that faithful teaching and preaching the good news will still amaze and convict and draw others to Christ. But it will also bring confrontation with those who do not really want to hear that the kingdom of *God* is near because it may require a giving up of what one has in status, power, and wealth; because it may threaten position; it may undermine a status quo that thinks God doesn't mind if we sell a few pigeons in the narthex, or whatever is the modern equivalent of letting our economic pursuits compromise our obedience to the God who made us, redeemed us, and calls us to a way of justice and righteousness and peace.

So there is where the ministry lies—in those strange paradoxes of Christian faith where good news assumes repentance, where power is manifest in weakness, where saving life is found in losing it, where the yoke and burden Christ offers is light and easy but cruciform in shape, and where the authority that comes from God will draw people unto Christ but may set us in harm's way. To just such a ministry in this place Christ has called his servant.

Called of God

Scripture Lesson: Jeremiah 1

W<small>E ARE HERE TO</small> carry out the final stages of a long process that leads today to the ordination of your pastor to the ministry of Christ in the Presbyterian Church. That process comprises various steps—a lot of study and education; examinations and Personal Information Forms; interviews with sessions, presbytery committees, pulpit nominating committees; and perhaps much of which I am not even aware, particularly with regard to the personal demands, anxieties, hopes, and joys that accompany the whole process. Underneath all that, however, is something very basic that must never be lost in the complexities and processes leading to ordination. It is the reality and primacy of *God's call to the ministry.*

Calling is not confined to the vocation of ministry. But it is *intrinsic* to the ministry, at least in the Reformed tradition, if not in most others. That is, we understand participation in the ordained ministry as not primarily a job or a contract. It is not something we are hired or even invited to do. Nor is it something that we simply decide or choose to do. However it may be experienced, the ministry is something into which we are called. We come to that conviction in various ways: some of them more like an actual calling, a self-conscious sense of being impelled into the ministry from beyond oneself; others more like a discernment that is rooted in one's self-assessment and self-understanding, one's openness to the world and the gospel. However that conviction may come, the ministry is created by the call of God and not finally by human decision.

For the sake of keeping this understanding of ordination before us, I would have us focus upon one of those texts of Scripture that speak quite explicitly about God's calling of a human being into God's service. In the Old Testament, that experience is tied most concretely to the calling of prophets. I realize one should be careful about too easily tying the call of those strange and difficult figures we know of as the prophets to any call to the ministry. But I would also say one should not be *too* careful and hesitant about seeing the connections. Aside from the fact that the prophetic role is a significant part of the work of the ministry—or should be—there is no experience of the call of God's servants in Scripture that is not capable of informing our own understanding of vocation, of calling, to the ministry.

That connection between the prophet's experience of God's call and our own is reinforced by the realization that there is a kind of sameness to all of these experiences of calling in the Old Testament, that to see Jeremiah's story is to hear about what happened with many others, and thus to discern some things that seem fundamental to the call of God's servants in different times and situations.

There are four dimensions to the call of God as exemplified in Jeremiah's account that I would lift up. Each of them is to be found again and again when we hear about how these prophets and leaders came to the position they occupied.

1.   Jeremiah's ministry is by divine appointment and election.

> Before I formed you in the womb I knew you,
>   and before you were born I consecrated you;
>   I appointed you a prophet to the nations. (Jer 1:5)

Jeremiah and his fellow prophets, or a Moses or a Gideon, did not assume their functions in God's governance and purpose out of a desire or a disposition or a particular bent for that sort of thing. The real decision is God's, not Jeremiah's. Here it is even expressed in a kind of election that belongs to his very being. His calling is not a happenstance. It is what he was born to be and to do by the very plan and intention of God. If Reformed Christians say with vigor and joy that we know ourselves, even before we were born, to have been elected into love, a story such as this lets us know that there were and are some who discover that they were, even before they were born, elected into vocation. There is nothing accidental about God's call, though it may be experienced "by accident" so to say. I am sure it was a big surprise to Jeremiah. And Amos lets us know that he had a very good vocation as a businessman before "the LORD took me from following after the flock and said, 'Go, prophesy to my people Israel.'"

2.   Amos's words as well as the account of Jeremiah's call underscore the second dimension of the call of God in these stories. *It is a calling to a*

task. And that means more to a task than to an office. Indeed, Jeremiah is appointed a prophet. People know what to call him. They know how to type him and associate him with other folks of similar stripe. The big deal, however, is not being a prophet, assuming a role. It is taking up a task. So Amos says: "The LORD took me [the divine election and appointment] and said, 'Go, prophesy to my people Israel'" (Amos 7:15). And Isaiah hears the words: "Whom shall I send and who will go for us?" (Isa 6:8) And to Jeremiah comes the command: "You shall go to all to whom I send you, and you shall speak whatever I command you" (Jer 1:7). Ministry means service. It is that dimension that we hear in these calls: the service of God under assignment. One may indeed speak of the prophet's mantle, of the descent of the spirit, of an anointing, ways of saying one now belongs to this category, to this group or office in God's kingdom. An identity is given thereby. But the identity is missional. What is most prominent is the sense of being commanded and sent and commissioned to do something.

3.   The third feature that stands out so prominently in Jeremiah's call, as well as in others about which we read, is that God's call places a burden upon the recipient that he or she (and there were women prophets) would prefer not to take up or does not feel able to handle: "Ah Lord GOD! Truly I do not know how to speak, for I am only a boy" (Jer 1:6). Moses raises a similar objection—among others. I don't speak well. We try to work on that in seminary. Those who don't speak well can learn to speak better. But the word is from God, and youthfulness has nothing to do with capacity for service. The prophet is empowered by God and given a word to speak by God. We must not, however, dismiss the kind of reluctance that Jeremiah and Moses and others express. It is probably quite appropriate. They probably did not have the proper capacities. They probably knew that the calling would be difficult and dangerous. But their disposition and capabilities and anxieties were not determining factors when under the call of God. Objection is to be expected and understandable. It is not finally effective as a resistance to the call of God.

4.   But that is at least in part because of the last of these shared features in the prophetic call stories. It is simply that one does not go into this difficult task without the assurance of God's protecting presence. A fearfulness before the task and the obstacles to the prophetic ministry is acknowledged. But that ministry is taken up under the divine

assurance: "Do not be afraid of them, for I am with you to deliver you" (Jer 1:8). It is finally only the failure to carry out the task that places a legitimate fear upon the prophet: "Gird up your loins. Stand up and tell them everything that I command you. Do not break down before them, or I will break you before them. And I for my part have made you today a fortified city, an iron pillar, and a bronze wall, against the whole land . . . They will fight against you, but they shall not prevail against you, for I am with you, says the LORD, to deliver you" (Jer 1:17–19) One does not stand under the prophetic call alone and without divine presence and support. The promise of that powerful presence belongs to the very calling that is given.

What then does all this mean for the call to the ministry? I trust that much of that is fairly obvious, but let me simply identify four implications that I see in the resonances between the call of the prophet and the call of the minister.

1. We are not in this business for and cannot claim status and power. Ordination is not the achievement of a particular status. It is the confirmation, in a public way, of your call. It is something special. And precisely because one senses that this is indeed God's call, one ought to have some sense of election, of being chosen, a special place. But that chosenness is for vocation and ministry, that special place is at the feet of disciples who are dirty and need washing not at the head of the table at the country club. This collar is not an award or even a credential. It is a yoke of service. The only thing that distinguishes the minister of the gospel from all others who carry out the ministry of Christ in the world is this calling to the preaching and pastoral ministry that is confirmed *by* the church and for the *sake* of the church.

2. That means, then—and this is my second inference—that with every particular decision about where and how we carry out this ministry, we do so in relation to the sense of God's call and not primarily in relation to features of the particular task of ministry, of the church or of the personal situation. That is not to say that we give no consideration to those matters. To ignore them is foolish. But they are not the final determinants in the decision. The reality of God's call means going where the Lord sends, not finding the best pastorate or teaching position.

That, of course, is not always easy to do. The Presbyterian Church has always understood that the call of God is not fully discerned until it is confirmed by the call of a particular congregation or ministry. And sometimes we do not hear or receive that call very easily. Here there is a rather sharp distinction from the prophetic call in that the call to the ministry is not finally a highly individual experience. It takes place in the community of faith. I do not finally know if God is calling me until others confirm that for me. Nor is it always the case that God sends us to those places that fit us well personally or professionally. It is difficult for me to conceive of Jeremiah or Ezekiel ever fitting well.

3. Indeed—and this is the third thing I hear in these call stories—if I read the prophetic calls correctly and if they are at all applicable to the experience of the call to the ministry, the sense that the job is too much or too difficult, or I do not have the abilities and capacities, or perhaps they will not listen to me—all of those are appropriate responses. If it all makes perfectly good sense or seems to be something that one would love to do, perhaps we ought to look a second time. If there is no objection in our minds and hearts, perhaps we are drawn to a position of ministry less by God's call than by the desirability of the position.

4. Finally—and happily this is the bottom line—there is no call of God that does not carry with it God's promise, a promise of God's presence and God's power. We do not go into this ministry alone. If it is true that God is always with us, these accounts of the prophetic calls tell us that is especially the case for those servants of the Lord who go where God has sent them to do the task that God has set. You *can* not do it alone. And we *do* not do it alone. We are not finally on our own. And so, the last word is not despair or fear. It is the promise of Emmanuel, the promise that when the congregation thinks you are too young, when your own efforts fail, when the burdens become too large to bear—and all of those things will happen—we are sustained and supported by the Lord who has called us into this ministry.

Advent and Christmas Time

Keep Awake

Scripture Lesson: Mark 13:32–39

Y OU ARE ALL FAMILIAR with the kind of prefatory note to a book that acknowledges the help of one or more people but then goes on to say that they are not responsible for any of the ways their material or counsel has been used in the present instance. I need to prefix one of those notes to this sermon. I owe a debt to Professor Donald Juel for his assistance in thinking about this text, but you cannot blame him for anything that follows.

To be honest, I owe him first of all for the text. When I was mumbling out loud about trying to decide what text to preach on this occasion, he reminded me (better, he *informed* me) that the text I have just read from the end of Mark 13 is one of the Advent texts and intimated that I might take a look at it. I wish he hadn't, and if you have listened to the text, you may wish the same. First of all, it is not an Old Testament text, which creates a problem from the start since, as you know, those are easier texts to preach. But then, I realized this is the conclusion of what is called the Little Apocalpyse in Mark. I thought that would help because, as you also know, if you can just give some label to a text—call it P or J or the Little Apocalpyse—you can distance it enough not to have to deal with it head on. But that didn't work. It simply intimidated me more. I don't know what to do with apocalyptic texts. Professor Sakenfeld and I always let one of our graduate teaching assistants handle the OT 101 lecture on apocalyptic. You don't think that is just accidental, do you? And, as you can easily detect, one of my homiletical strategies this morning—and it is a fairly common one—is to see how long I can go with this sermon without confronting the text.

The problem is that once Professor Juel stuck this text in my head, I couldn't shake it loose. So I am stuck with it—and now you have to join me in my predicament. For that much you can blame Professor Juel—but for no more than that.

At the risk of exegetical reductionism, I am going to suggest that the text has one word to say and two contexts in which that word is to be heard. First, the one word. It is not hard to spot. It is repeated again and again here—and only occurs one other place in this Gospel—and we will come to that in a moment. The one word occurs entirely in the imperative mood, that is, as a command or an exhortation. Which means we don't have to figure out if the word is relevant. It is very direct. That's the nice thing about commands in the biblical text. You know they are directed at somebody. You just have to figure out at whom the finger is being pointed.

The one word of the text is: "Keep awake!" There is a parable here as well, but its implication is not obscure. And its point is to clarify the repeated exhortation: "Keep awake." Keep awake, because you do not know when the time will come. What time? Keep awake because you don't know what time the master of the house is going to come home. Keep awake, lest the master come back and find you asleep. At one point, Jesus puts it: Sleep out in the open. It is that urgent to keep awake, and it may take lying on the open ground to do it.

The story Jesus tells is about a man who leaves home to go on a trip and leaves things in the charge or under the authority of all his servants "each with his work to do." And the doorkeeper especially has to keep awake to let the master in. There is a double warning implicit in the repeated command to keep awake. The most obvious and perhaps the most crucial is: Keep awake, so that you will be ready to receive your master. You do not want to be asleep and unable to greet the Lord who has been gone but now has come back. It is the Lord, of course, whose return is meant. That is the point of the whole chapter. But lest there be any uncertainty, when Jesus refers to the master of the house, it is the *kurios*, the *Lord*, of the house of whom he speaks. The point is twofold: You don't know when the Lord of the house is going to return, and you want to be ready to greet and welcome him whenever that happens.

A second warning in the exhortation to keep awake is *not to fall asleep on the job*. That is surely the case with the doorkeeper, who has to let the master in. But the references to the servants who are left with authority and each with his job to do suggests even further that one is to keep awake to tend to the tasks that are their responsibility. The Lord of the house is gone, but there is work to be done. It is demanding work; one may tire—one *will* tire. The absence of the Lord does not mean a vacation. Quite the contrary, while he is gone, the servants are in charge and have the power. It is up to them to stay at the work that is to be done without the oversight of the Lord of the house. The temptation, and it is all too human and real a temptation, would be to relax and let things go. When the Lord returns, we will greet him and do what he says. But the Lord has left things in our charge—excuse me—has left things in the *servants'* charge. There are tasks for each of us to do—excuse me—each of them to do in the meanwhile. These are the disciples who are to be left in charge until the Lord of the house returns. But, of course, this is the church that is in view, and if I have to point that out for you to see it, then we have large problems starting with not hearing the text, which ends, and not very subtly, with the words: "And what I say to you (the disciples) I say to *all*: Keep awake."

The meaning of Jesus's words to his disciples is not exhausted by their context, but they are certainly opened up in a particular and forceful way by what follows. We read in the next verses, which open chapter 14: "It was two days before the Passover and the festival of Unleavened Bread. The chief priests and the scribes were looking for a way to arrest Jesus by stealth and kill him." We are now into the story of the passion and death of Jesus. And we begin to see that the possible hours when the lord of the house might come back: "in the evening, or at midnight, or at cockcrow, or at dawn" are not accidental. That is not lunch time or 4:30 in the afternoon when the work is done. These times have a clearly double meaning. They are the times when folk are likely to be asleep, for that matter when they should be asleep! The hard and demanding word of this text cannot be glossed over. Some of us have trouble keeping awake at 1:30 in the afternoon, but at least that is expected. The word of the Lord here is that his coming may be when sleepy Christians have gone to bed and called it quits. Keep awake. But these times also give us a chronology for all that follows in the next chapter: The disciples gather with Jesus for Passover "in the evening." Jesus goes with his disciples into the garden in the middle of the night and they fall asleep. And we all know the significance of the cockcrow in the morning. Peter finally wakes up and stays up long enough to deny his Lord three times. And then at the beginning of chapter 15 we hear that "*As soon as it was dawn*, the chief priests held a consultation . . . and they bound Jesus, led him away, and handed him over to Pilate."

Before his coming there is his going. The disciples think that all that lies ahead are clouds of glory. And so they fall asleep, unaware of the dangers that lie ahead, unaware that their Lord is in anguish and afraid to death. Echoing the three occurrences in our text in the preceding chapter, Jesus now says three times to his disciples in the dark of night: Keep awake! But this time it is not a piece of teaching and instruction. It is a repeated plea that they stand with him in his agony and despair and in his prayer. And of course, they do not. And here is where the hard saying comes; here is where the text crushes us but cannot be tossed away. This is midnight. Mere human beings grow tired and belong asleep at that time of night. Don't rebuke the disciples unless you are prepared to keep awake with your Lord in the hour of trial and testing, unless you can resist the human need for rest. Don't blame them. At least don't you blame them, for you know their limits. Yet Jesus does blame them and rebukes them. And when he finds them asleep the third time, he says, "Enough, The hour has come; the Son of Man is betrayed into the hands of sinners." Our text says, "No one knows the hour but the father." Is this the hour of his coming? It would seem to be so. And this is not quite the promised glory with disciples sitting at the right hand and the left. The church that awaits the coming in glory and does not know when that time is but must keep at its work learns about keeping awake when it seems impossible in the garden with its Lord.

So is that what this text means for *Advent*? Now you see why I would rather pass this text by in the season of our anticipation of the coming one. I did not know that we had to deal with his going and our falling asleep when he needed us. I didn't even know he ever needed us, much less that we couldn't even stay awake to pray and suffer with him.

That is the hard word of the text, and we dare not let it slip from our hand. But that is not the last word of the text. It still is about the coming of the Lord and about keeping awake. And the church knows that coming is not simply past. Sleepy and despairing disciples could not believe that he had come in resurrection, but so he came. The church was startled into life as the Spirit of Christ blew among it and still does. So, we still do not know the hour. And the danger of falling asleep and missing his coming lies before us. Our Advent text is somewhat counterintuitive to the way we celebrate Advent. We do so in expectation because we know the day of his coming. It is Christmas! No you do not, says the Gospel. No you do not! So keep awake! Sleep out in the open if you have to, but keep awake.

Oh, I almost forgot. There is a small textual note at the bottom of the page. It says after the first time Jesus says, "Keep awake," that "Other ancient authorities add *and pray*." Some textual notes make all the difference in the world. I would adopt that one if I were you.

Joy to the World

Old Testament Lesson: Isaiah 41:8–10; 52:7–10
New Testament Lesson: Matthew 1:18–25; Luke 2:8–20

I HOPE YOU LISTENED carefully to the four texts you have just heard. There are a lot of other good texts in the Bible. There are a lot more things God has to say to you in the pages of Scripture. There are a lot more things you need to hear about how to lead your life and how to help me and others lead ours. But if it is the gospel you want to hear, if it is the good news that addresses poor folk out in the field, desolate and exiled folk captive in a foreign world. If you want to know what is the piece of really good news that is for *all people*, then you just heard it and you don't need any more text. In fact you don't need any more *words*. You just need to soak those words up, take them to heart, and praise the Lord!

But we are here and we have another fifteen minutes, and maybe it won't hurt to soak these words up together, to think about them and what they mean to us. There certainly isn't anything better I will ever have to talk to you about in class or out.

The text from the book of Isaiah is one of the many oracles of salvation that ring throughout the Old Testament. It is the gospel form of Scripture, Old Testament and New. That is, it is the summary or epitome of the good news that God has declared throughout history and that rings so loudly once more in this Advent season on the eve of our Saviour's birth. It is very simple and very basic: "You don't have to be afraid."

Whenever in Israel's story the people or individuals lifted to God their plight and suffering, the deepest fears and their momentary fears, there came again and again the basic assuring message: Don't be afraid. Abraham heard it when he feared he would have no child. Hagar heard it in the wilderness afraid that she and her child were about to die. Jacob heard it as he faced his brother Esau, whom he had cheated. Hezekiah heard it in the face of the Assyrian threat at the gates of Jerusalem. Exiles in Babylon heard it in the very depths of discouragement. "Do not be afraid; I am with you; I will help you." It was a word that served to turn their despair into confidence, their terrible weariness into renewed strength. The prophet said it was like folks who have nothing but raggedy old clothes suddenly finding themselves in a brand new dress from Lord and Taylor and a cool new cashmere sports coat from Brooks Brothers! (That's what we call in exegesis a *dynamic* translation.) People who had not been able to do anything but cry out their complaints and laments now found themselves singing and shouting for joy.

The good news of great joy that we hear from the angels each Christmas is the same word. At Jesus's birth came the assurance again: "Fear not." Phillips Brooks said it correctly in his familiar carol about Bethlehem: "The hopes and fears of all the years are met in thee tonight." And in that meeting fears are changed to hopes through the demonstration of God's love in Jesus. Matthew tells us that the names of the child of Bethlehem declare to all who see him that he embodies the will and purpose of a gracious God. For he is Immanuel, God with us, a sign and demonstration that the power that creates and undergirds the universe is truly among us in the most intimate personal way. And the angel said, Call him Jesus, which means he will save his people from their sins. He is God in our midst and for us, to help and to save. His love and compassion, his justice and mercy, his identification with us and selfless giving for us—all of that is God's way with us. So do not be afraid. That is the good tidings brought in the birth of this child. And it is good news for you, not just for somebody else. There isn't a soul in this room who does not need and want to hear that word.

I am sure that many of you know Frederick Buechner's wonderful little book *Wishful Thinking*, which he subtitles *A Theological ABC*. In it, he writes these words:

> A crucial eccentricity of the Christian faith is the assertion that people are saved by grace. There's nothing *you* have to do. There's nothing you *have* to do. There's nothing you have to *do*.
>
> The grace of God means something like: Here is your life. You might never have been, but you *are* because the party wouldn't have been complete without you. Here is the world. Beautiful and terrible things will happen. Don't be afraid. I am with you. Nothing can ever separate us. It's for you I created the universe. I love you.[1]

---

1. Buechner, *Wishful Thinking*, 34.

As we read about God's good news to us in the Bible, there are some things that seem to be very characteristic of it there. I believe they are dimensions of the good news for us also.

1. One is that the loving relationship between God and humankind that is made visible in Jesus's coming and articulated in the promise that you don't have to be afraid is not a theological abstraction. It signifies that our relationship to the one who is the source and ground of all life and all things is not cold and impersonal but intimate, personal, and caring. To each of us individually the assurance is given. You don't have to fear. I am with *you*. I am for *you*.

2. A second characteristic of the promise and assurance of God's care and help is that it calls forth a response of faith and trust, of confidence in the promise of God despite outward appearances and present reality. When exiles heard the words not to be afraid, God would help them, they had to trust that word because when it came to them, nothing at that point had changed. And all the aura and grandeur of the Christmas season makes it easy for us to forget the utter anonymity and insignificance of the birth of the child Jesus in an out-of-the-way place. He came in a time of Roman rule and oppression. When he died, that situation had not changed. The world neither then nor now is harmonious and fear free. Before his life was over, he would weep over the city of Jerusalem, crying out in anguish: "Would that you knew the things that belong to your peace!" What would he say now if he saw the fires burning on the Via Dolorosa and the stones and bullets and rockets hurled through the air? How can one see any way out? Only, I venture to say, by trust in the assurance of God, in God's promise to be with us and to help, realizing that standing in the shadows of the manger is a hill named Golgotha with a cross on it, that God's way to help us through the child Jesus is for *God* a way through pain and suffering, a demonstration that even, indeed especially, in those moments God is with us.

3. Finally, to hear the words "Don't be afraid" is to turn from fear and sadness and anxiety to joy and exultation. The exiles' laments by the waters of Babylon turned into hymns of praise and joy—while they still sat by those same waters. The shepherds, who are, in this story, the poor of the earth—don't glamorize them with fancy bathrobes in your Christmas pageants—turned from fear to praise and glorify God

because of the good news of a savior—even as they walked back to their cold, hard life in the fields outside Bethlehem. That is because they were confident that despite all the counterindicators around them, God was working in the world with them and for them. The joy of the Christmas season is a reflection of that same joy, the result of our confidence that the birth of Jesus is the fulfillment of God's promise to be with us so that we need never fear again.

In recent days I have come across a Christmas letter from some close friends of ours, written now a quarter of a century ago. I came across it because periodically I get it out at Christmas time to remind me of what this celebration is all about. It has helped me understand, and so I venture to share it with you. The letter was written by our next-door neighbors eight months after they had suffered terrible pain and grief at the tragic and inexplicable suicide of their teenage son. I do not know if I could have written these words, but I receive them again and again as the gospel. After thanking their many friends for support in the months of their sorrow, they concluded with these words: "The declaration of Christmas is that by God's grace there is light for our darkness, hope for our despair, peace for our chaos, and that the long night of sorrow has been turned into the morning light of joy." And then a small handwritten addition: "What more is there to say?" I can't think of anything else, can you? As another friend once said to me: God had it all—and gave it all away—to us. So don't be afraid.

Christmas:

The Surprising Imagination of God[1]

Scripture Lessons: Luke 1:46–55; 2:1–20

IF WE SAY OF someone, "What an imagination!" we could mean several things, but we usually are trying to say that such-and-such a person thinks about things in a far-out sort of way, is able to come up with ideas, stories, and dreams that others of us may not have. We are probably not accustomed to thinking of God as having an imagination. With God we think of other characteristics, such as those of which Mary speaks in the Magnificat: God's power, holiness, and mercy. But Christmas and the stories, the words, the events of Christmas are a demonstration of the marvelous imagination of God, in the sense of the mind set loose to think and plan, to act in different ways. Everything about Christmas is so familiar to us that it is difficult for any of it to surprise us and evoke the responses of those surprised by God—that may be why we give gifts, because they can evoke the responses of that marvelous hoped-for but unexpected gift of that first Christmas.

The Christmas story, despite its familiarity, is full of surprises, as God's story with the Lord's people has always been. And all of the surprises are aspects of a single wonder—that when *God* does things, greatness is found in the midst of the lowly; what matters most takes shape in and among what most of us would think matters little or not at all. That is what the Christmas story is about from beginning to end. Mary declares it, and the story dramatizes it: that in the baby born in a tiny corner of the world "the hopes and fears of all the years are met" and turn into songs of joy that echo

---

1. Parts of this sermon were later drawn upon in two of the author's editorial essays in the journal *Theology Today*, Miller, "The Church's First Theologian," 72–76; and Miller, "January's Child," 98–102, reprinted in Miller, *Theology Today*, 72–76 and 98–102.

down through the centuries and are sung again and again, that the God who is Lord of all, the transcendent mystery beyond our comprehension, the ground of all that is, takes shape in our midst in an unknown child, son of a Jewish carpenter from a place in the Galilean hills called Nazareth. Not exactly what I would have thought up to accomplish the ultimate purposes of God. But then I would hardly have imagined the savior of the world born in a barn on a straw mattress. It may look romantic in a Christmas tableaux, but no mother-to-be would choose such crude, uncomfortable, and threatening circumstances in which to bring forth her child. Yet it is *in* the crude, uncomfortable, and threatening that God places God's own child with all the risks and none of the fanfare—except in heaven. A birth announcement goes out—but not to the great, the important, the religious and secular leaders of the country. It goes to lowly inhabitants of the area, busy with other matters, trying to earn a simple living. It came as a startling surprise to those shepherds.

In Mary's song of praise at the announcement of her child to be, she tells us that God really does imagine things in a quite different way from the normal run of things, that the great among the lowly and the lowly among the great is God's way with the world (vv. 51–53). Does this mean simply a reversal: the powerless become powerful, the rich become poor and vice versa? I doubt it. That is the way we think of revolutions—the weak take power from the mighty and the poor take the wealth of the rich. The end result is too often more of the same, only the roles are reversed. But that is the problem with *our limited* imaginations. In the birth of Jesus, however, God outruns our imagination. Mary's words in her Magnificat are to be taken seriously, a clue to what this Christmas business is all about—things do not work in the way we expect and accept when God's purpose, God's imagination, is underway. The proud and self-sufficient who show no need of God or God's help shall not rule and run things in the kingdom that is ruled by the stable-born, manger-laid, shepherd-watched baby; and the lowly, those who cannot trust in their own strength because they have none and have to rely in utter confidence upon God, shall be exalted. But that exaltation of the weak, and the great and rich becoming low and poor, may surprise us even more.

It is beyond my imagination—though I see a few clues that are given here that are indeed surprising. The primary one is Mary herself, unheralded, of no claim to fame, wife of a Jewish carpenter, truly one of low estate who regards herself as handmaid of the Lord and sees that in choosing her

God has exalted her to high estate. Mary gains no wealth or power in the worldly sense. Yet in and through this humble woman, God's great purpose shall come to pass. Mary, you see, not Herod or Caesar, is God's revolutionary, imaginative way.

And the sharpest clue is in the way that will be shown by the baby in the stable, who though he was in the form of God did not count equality with God—power, high estate—a thing to be grasped . . . but humbled himself and became obedient unto death, the way of this child who though he was rich yet for our sakes became poor. Therefore, God has highly exalted him (from Phil 2:5–9).

One further word. If Christmas points us to such a revolutionary, transforming, imaginative power at work in our world, how do we respond to that? Our focus upon Christmas is on getting ready for it, on waiting for the coming of the child. But how to react when Christmas is here, and the child who signals and keeps God's way in the world has come? Well, the clues are there, this time clearly in the story. One of the reactions is spontaneous praise, Mary's Magnificat Anima Mea: "My soul magnifies the Lord"; the shepherds' return home no longer fear-filled but glorifying and praising God. To hear of the birth of this child—as we do—and what it means is also to marvel, wonder, to be amazed and surprised as were those who heard the shepherds' report. And there is a further reaction that goes long beyond the days of Christmas. It is the response of Mary, who pondered all these things in her heart. I suspect she mulled them over on the flight to Egypt, wondering how her precious baby could provoke such terrible and destructive rage from King Herod. I am sure that many years later as she watched the agonizing death of her child, she pondered through tears how God had exalted God's lowly handmaid and what that required of her.

That's what the story says, and those clues probably are appropriate to *our* story. For surely the carol-filled season is no accident. Music truly fills the air as at no other times, and the sound is praise—all our joyous carols picking up the Magnificat of Mary and Bach, the Gloria of angels on high and of choirs in cathedrals and churches of every sort. We hear the praises of shepherds and children, of monks and carolers who stop by the door of the sick, the needy, the old, to praise the God whose imagination turns things all around with a baby in a Judean village. And look into the eyes of all those children around you in these days to find afresh the wonder and joyous surprise at this moment of God's doing. For no season of our life evokes more wonder and surprise than this one.

And when it is all over, and even now as you come to the table of the Lord, do as Mary did—and after her, theologians and preachers, other mothers and fathers, Christians everywhere; think with care about what it is that God did at Christmas. Nothing is ever the same again.

Funeral Services

Precious in the Sight of the Lord
(Psalm 116:15)[1]

THERE IS NO ESCAPING the loss and grief that are ours this morning in the face of the death of Lila Bonner Miller. But that is surely not the primary or dominant emotion in our hearts. For if ever there was a time for thanksgiving and praise, this is it. Her children, at least, and her grandchildren—and I am sure there are many more—know that our lives have been shaped and blessed and gifted beyond measure by the presence and the words and deeds of the one we call Mother and Grandmother and others call Lila and Dr. Miller. There was nothing more sure to her than the grace and providence of God in her life, and she has made that grace and providence sure for us. "Bless the LORD, O my soul, and forget not all his benefits." And she never did. I suppose somewhere along the way we came to realize that those words were not just something we had to memorize as we read and learned the 103rd Psalm on Sunday afternoons in our childhood. They were the truth; they were the reality that sustains our lives. "Come, O children, listen to me; I will teach you the fear of the LORD." And she did, so that none of us can ever live apart from the fear of the Lord. For her patients as much as for herself and her children, the one thing she knew could be counted upon to uphold us in the face of everything else is the conviction that "You are a child of God." There was no therapy more effective and no motherly wisdom more important than that conviction.

---

1. This sermon was preached at the funeral service for Dr. Lila Bonner Miller at the Druid Hills Presbyterian Church in Atlanta, Georgia, in September 1995.

While there is much to her life and work that stands out, I expect that nothing will remain with us more than our sense of her as someone who was always teaching.

If Mother was teaching us continually, it was only because she was herself always learning, always interested in new things, eager to read everything. In her small bedroom in her apartment, there were three bookcases, and books piled up all over the floor. As she grew older, she would often ask whoever was there among her children to come lie down on the bed with her and visit. That was fine, except there was usually very little room on the bed because books were littered all over it. At the age of eighty-six she visited us in Boston in the context of attending a continuing education seminar on neurology. She became a kind of theological groupie attending courses and lectures that Walter [Brueggemann] and I and others gave at various places. She pored over books on the brain and books on God, read nearly every book that Walter has written, no small feat. But she read her Bible and knew it better than any of the other books.

This unceasing desire to learn was manifest in various ways. It showed up in her openness to the new and to change. She was not afraid of change and taught us not to be. She said change was natural. What mattered was what you did with it. For one so steeped in the tradition of her faith and her family, she was truly open to new ideas and unafraid to challenge the set ways and assumptions of the past. Her openness to the new was present even in such simple things as learning games. She loved games and was always eager to learn a new one. I think she was far more inventive for us in our childhood than we were later on for our own children. Mother could also get tickled and laugh so hard the tears rolled down. I think one of the most difficult things for me about her stroke at eighty-nine was that the laughter no longer came readily. She loved jokes but often did not catch on. Last night we remembered the time that we were playing that game where you think up a pair of rhyming words and give the others a definition to see if they can guess your rhyme—"stinky pinkies," we called them rather inelegantly. An obese feline, for example, would be a "fat cat." We were throwing these around right and left and guessing each others rhymes fairly easily. Mother finally jumped in and said, "I have one. It is something good to eat." We all came up with several rhymed words of something good to eat. But she just sat there shaking her head with this big grin on her face at our stupidity. Finally, in exasperation, we said, "We give up. What is it?" She smiled even more broadly and said, "Fried fish." She was so proud of having stumped her children and grandchildren that I don't think she ever realized that she had not caught on to the game.

But all of that was apart of her zest for life, something that we all will recall in many images: from her sitting on the bank of the Nueces River with a bamboo pole to her stirring the fish she caught in a big skillet out in the hot Texas sun. She loved to eat—anything. All of us children have images of the Montreat porch, or back porch literally, covered with bushel and half-bushel baskets of fruit and vegetables after she had made a trip to the Farmer's Market in Asheville. Her grandchildren would sit fascinated as she ate her fried chicken, not only down to the bone but right on through, chewing up bones and all. And there are other images that tell us something about this woman and the kind of stuff of which she was made: curing half a hog on the back porch of the Druid Hills [Presbyterian Church, Atlanta] manse; gutting, skinning, and cutting up a deer when Mr. Parker brought one to the manse in San Antonio on the last day of deer season with just us three children to help her, only to find two hours later our father coming in with great pride with a deer and a turkey. They cleaned them both and twenty minutes later were on their way to a big wedding at First Presbyterian Church.

Her son-in-law, George [McMaster], properly saw in her last words to him a kind of parable of her life. When he told her it was time to go eat supper, she said, "Well, I need to do something!" One of her friends wrote to the family after her death that whatever the Communion of Saints has been up to until now, it is going to be different with Lila aboard.

Mother taught us all, directly and indirectly, by example and by instruction. She made us learn Scripture and gave us rules for life from traditional proverbs, such as "many hands make light work," to her own rules, such as "everybody works and everybody gets an education." She took whatever measure necessary to get us to learn. One summer she offered me a quarter for every poem I would learn. With her grandchildren, she upped the ante. One summer she offered *five dollars* to any of them who would learn the books of the Bible. They learned them with alacrity, of course, but that was not the end of it. All their friends learned about this gold mine, went to their Bibles, and then came by the house to recite the books of the Bible and get their five dollars.

There were three particular areas where I think Mother was always teaching us:

For one, she taught us how to be women and men and to be men and women together. That was evident in her relationship with Father. How could two people be more different! But she was devoted to her husband, and we learned from that. She wanted her son to know the things that belonged to being a man—but to be careful. And she wanted her daughters to know and to do more than women often tended to do—but to be cagey. She took great pride in the achievements, the competence, and the commitments of her daughters, Belle and Mary, to their family, their work, and their church.

But her instruction was not confined to her daughters. New members of the family also came under her particular kind of tutelage. I remember a formative moment in our marriage relationship the first summer after Mary Ann and I were married and were visiting with the family in Montreat for a week. We were sitting around the table after lunch when Mary Ann said that she would like a cup of coffee. She then turned to me and asked if I would like one also. I said that I would. But as she rose to go get the coffee, Mother grabbed her arm, pulled her back down in her seat, and said, "Are you going to wait on him the rest of your life?" The lesson, of course, was as much for me as it was for Mary Ann.

That story is typical also of her assertive manner that was sometimes in your face but mostly to the point in ways that got to the heart of the matter. She was direct but rarely unkind. She said what she thought, and most of the time what she thought was something helpful, even if difficult for others to hear. On one of our last visits to her in the nursing home, when she had pretty much quit talking and would just sit there while we talked around her, I noticed that she had a copy of a book I had written recently; Mary, whose compassionate care of Mother over the last seven years is beyond what any of us will ever know, had gotten her the book. Always trying to get a response of some sort, I said, "I see you have my book." No response. So I said, not really expecting any response, "What did you think of it?" Then, after a brief moment, came a quiet, "Too long"—which was exactly the kind of direct and truthful response Mother always gave.

A second thing she taught us was to care about others and especially people in trouble or in need. The Druid Hills Community Fellowship, which she started, is the primary testimony to her care of others, and she never let any of her family visit on a Sunday evening without being roped in to participate and help out. Her medical practice was a further demonstration of her concern for the sick and suffering. Indeed her whole life was built on the assumption that you helped people who needed help. Hospitality to strangers was as natural to her as breathing. Belle recalled how during our years of growing up, there was never a Sunday dinner when there were not strangers at the dinner table, some of whom became friends. Surely Mother hears now the words of the king: "I was hungry and you gave me food . . . I was a stranger and you welcomed me . . . I was sick and you took care of me" (Matt 25:35–36).

And finally she taught us how to grow old. That, of course, was in a sense the whole point of the documentary, *Lila*, which was filmed when she was eighty. But there she was still a robust, active woman. I expect it was in these last seven years, as she lay in a nursing home after a major stroke, that she did her most important teaching about how to stay alive even when there is not much there, how to be human to the end. As long as she could, she kept reading; as long as she could she kept painting. On her last visit away from the nursing home, she stayed several days in our home in Montreat. Every night I would go in to check her as she lay in bed, and she would be reading and underlining her copy of Karl Barth's *Göttingen Dogmatics* until she fell asleep.

And till the end, she directed her heart and her mind to the one she knew above all else loved her and would hold her forever. At her burial, these words were read from Romans 14. Here Paul is surely speaking about Lila:

> We do not live to ourselves, and we do not die to ourselves.
> If we live, we live to the Lord, and if we die, we die to the Lord;
> so then, whether we live or whether we die, we are the Lord's. (vv. 7–8)

In the years after our father died, Mother carried on as fully as ever, but she missed him beyond imagining. One verse came to be a sort of touchstone for her, and I heard her repeat it often in the apartment on Jamestown Road. It is from the 116th Psalm:

> Precious in the sight of the LORD is the death of his saints. (v. 15)

It was a kind of fundamental assurance to her, that the man she loved so dearly was even more dearly loved by her Master and was, beyond death, precious in God's sight. So now she leaves those words of the psalmist with us. It is fitting that the psalmist give the yea and amen to the life of this remarkable woman of faith, for the psalms were the voice that most clearly spoke for her. In her last months, her own voice was almost silent. Yet, three words returned again and again to her lips or were written over and over again on her pad—she always had a book, a writing pad, and her magnifying glass. The words were "trust and obey." Those words are from an old hymn, of course, but they are at the heart of the life of faith as the Psalms proclaim it. At ninety-five, when it would seem that she could now simply let go, she was reminding herself of what it meant to fear the Lord. Trust and obey. She did that, and because she did, we will probably do so better than we would have had she not been among us.

Heaven[1]

NOT LONG AGO, WHEN Mary Ann and I were visiting with her mother, she asked me what I thought about heaven. I was taken aback at the time because my mind was, as usual, on more mundane things than that. I don't recall what response I made at the time, except that it was not very helpful. But the question was a serious one from this ninety-year-old woman whose husband had died some years before. It has stuck with me ever since and in these few minutes I would like to take it up again with a bit more reflection.

Heaven really has two connotations in Christian faith. One is spatial—up there—and one is temporal—beyond death. In the first instance, heaven is *a symbol for God's reality and God's rule*. It is a pointer to transcendence, to the fact that what we mean by God is one who is above and beyond all that we are even if among us.

Heaven is a biblical and Christian way of speaking about the abode of God. Some of you are old enough to remember when the Russian premier Nikita Kruschchev scoffed at the notion of God and heaven when he noted that the Russian astronauts had not seen God or heaven when they went into space. His mockery reflects a widespread tendency to literalize the notion of heaven, when in fact it is a symbol and not a literal reality, at least as described in the Bible. As a symbol, however, it points to something real, but something we can only think of in images and pictures because it is beyond us, and we do not have direct experience of it.

The symbol of heaven thus tells us several things. It tells us that our lives are not determined and shaped and delimited by what we can see or touch or explore or know. It tells us that this chaotic world of hurricanes and tsunamis and wars and death in all its manifold forms, which is what we see so much, is not a meaningless, haphazard thing out there but is the

1. This sermon was preached on September 6, 2005, at the funeral service of George R. McMaster at the Druid Hills Presbyterian Church in Atlanta, Georgia.

creation of God, who rules in the midst of both human chaos and natural disaster. That is, Scripture speaks easily about the "kingdom of God" and the "kingdom of heaven." To speak of heaven is to claim that God is real and God rules all that is, apart from which our present life borders on meaninglessness and hopelessness.

But heaven has another connotation for Christian faith. It is a symbol for the conviction that our final destiny is in God's care. Here also, the symbol is often characterized by images that are meant to connote and point to the reality, because we have to speak in pictures of some sort. So we speak of "pearly gates" and "streets of gold." "Streets of gold" is only a way of saying that heaven is better than anything we know, but we can only say that by using earthly images—images that are inadequate the minute we use them. I think I remember Mother Sudduth being singularly unimpressed with the prospect of streets of gold as a part of her or anybody else's future. Even the notion of place that is indicated by the term heaven is inadequate, because it is not place as we know any notion of place.

What matters in all of this is the Christian claim—and I believe it to be true with all my heart—that we are forever held in the arms of God. That is true before we were born; that will be true after we have died and our bodies have disappeared. Who and what we are still lives with God and is kept by God. That is what is meant by eternal life. We talk about immortality of the soul, resurrection of the body, and the like, but we cannot really know what those terms mean. They are beyond our experience. That does not mean, however, that they do not point to something that is true and real. They are ways of saying that God completes our lives beyond this life, whether we have died young or old, have suffered or lived well. Underneath, now and forever, are the everlasting arms, and they will keep us. An image again, of course, but it is where I hope and believe I will be and you will be. And after New Orleans I know all the more "the everlasting arms" is a better image than the streets, whether they are made of gold or full of water. Death is real, but it really is not the last word. As God knew us and kept us before we were born, so the same will be beyond this life and its death.

That is a claim that George McMaster made for himself and for us in his choice of Psalm 139 as one of the texts to be read as we remember his life and hope for his resurrection.

For it was you who formed my inward parts.
You knit me together in my mother's womb.
I praise you, for I am fearfully and wonderfully made.
Wonderful are your works;
that I know very well.
My frame was not hidden from you,
when I was being made in secret,
intricately woven in the depths of the earth.
Your eyes beheld my unformed substance.
In your book were written
all the days that were formed for me.
when none of them as yet existed.
How weighty to me are your thoughts, O God!
How vast is the sum of them!
I try to count them—they are more than sand;
I come to the end—I am still with you.

(vv. 13–18)

God is far beyond our comprehension; so also heaven and the future. What we know and hear afresh in the psalm is whatever end there is, when we come to it, we are still with God, still kept and held. As our beginning was with God, so will our end be as well.

If heaven is a symbol of spatial and temporal significance, it is also a highly relational symbol, and this is a part of the Christian hope and confidence about the future that seems to mean more and more to me as the years go by. It is what the church means by the communion of saints. That is a way of speaking about the fellowship of all who have lived as a part of the community of faith. It is also a way of saying that as our lives have been lived together, whatever is beyond that continues that relationship. The image that is most helpful to me and comes to mind again and again is the picture at the beginning of Hebrews 12: "Since we are surrounded by so great a cloud of witnesses . . ." I see in my mind that cloud of witnesses every time I sing "The Church's One Foundation" and come to that verse: "Yet she on earth hath union with God the three in one; / and mystic sweet communion with those whose rest is won."

I really do believe that in some way George, and our fathers and mothers, our grandfathers and grandmothers, and all those who have gone before surround us even now and keep us and bear witness to us beyond their life. And whatever we have known of loving relationship is not lost. How we shall experience that relationship beyond our death, we do not know. But it belongs to whatever future with God that we have. I know that the climax of 1 Corinthians 13 is meant to be the final verse. For me, however, it comes at the end of Paul's characterization of love and all that it means with those concluding three words: "Love never ends."

And since we are indeed surrounded by so great a cloud of witnesses, let us, as the writer to the Hebrews says, run the race that is set before us. Their example, their faith, their holding on is an enduring testimony that calls us to persevere no matter what the future may hold. Heaven means that the future itself is held secure, which is why Christian hope is conviction and not wishful thinking.

I cannot prove any of this, but I do not believe that we are misled by the gospel and the church's experience. Christian hope is not desperate. It is trusting and reliable. It is real and means we can take what comes in this world knowing that the God who is with us now will keep us forever and make our lives full.

We Are the Lord's[1]

Old Testament Lesson: Psalm 139:1–18

New Testament Lesson: Romans 14:7–9 [5–9]

IN ONE OF HIS last essays, titled "Christian Hope and the Denial of Death," Don Juel argued, with his usual vigor, that "the real barrier to the birth of Christian hope is not the idea of resurrection . . . but the denial of death."[2] In these last weeks, he came to know personally what he had learned from the New Testament. Now he has forced us to take his point with ultimate seriousness.

It is just such a mixture of candor and hope that erupts from the Apostle Paul in the midst of his trying to deal with what someone has described as a family feud over church supper menus. In the midst of fussing with the Romans over their eating habits, he says these words:

> We do not live to ourselves, and we do not die to ourselves. If we live, we live to the Lord, and if we die, we die to the Lord; so then, whether we live or whether we die, we are the Lord's. For to this end Christ died and lived again, so that he might be Lord of both the dead and the living. (Rom 14:7–9)

It is difficult to escape his point, reinforced so many times in such a short space: We are the Lord's. That is the bottom line of all bottom lines. But what does it mean that we are the Lord's? I take it that means several things. Clearly from the discussion that precedes, it means that all our practices, however different they may be—Lutheran or Presbyterian, chanting or speaking, observance or nonobservance, receiving the elements or

---

1. This sermon was preached on March 1, 2003, at the funeral service of Donald H. Juel at the Nassau Presbyterian Church in Princeton, New Jersey.

2. Juel, "Christian Hope," 174.

coming to the table—all of our practices are to the honor and glory of God, and that is what matters.

But it is clear from the way this Scripture breaks out of the realm of practice to a larger reality, that there is something more basic in the declaration that we are the Lord's. And that is the way in which this claim challenges the most fundamental understanding of our humanness. For we assume the great divide every human being faces is that between life and death. All other distinctions are subordinate to that.

According to the Scriptures, however, *at one crucial point*, there is no distinction between life and death. Living or dying, living *and* dying, we belong to the Lord; there is no difference about that, whatever our state. There really is something deeper than our life and death that undergirds both and transcends both. We are the Lord's. Earlier, Paul makes the same point when he says that neither death nor life can separate us from the love of God in Christ Jesus. The seal on that claim is the knowledge that, as our text puts it, Christ died and lived again.

Psalm 139 also speaks of this conviction that we are the Lord's, and in two ways. First is in the realization of the *inescapability* of God, that there is no experience, nothing we can do, nothing we can attempt, no place we can go that can take us away from the presence of God. Like the poet pursued by the hound of heaven, wherever we go, we are pursued by the one whom we call Lord. The psalmist knows that is not always a pleasant reality. Sometimes the hand of the Lord lies heavy upon us. Finally, however, it is what we count on, to be held fast and led by the Lord's hand into whatever lies before us.

And so the psalmist draws a picture of God knitting us and weaving us into being long before our birth, long before there was any idea of our being. When we read this psalm together one day, Don said to Lynda, "Tell him about Limburg's sermon." And so Lynda told of a baptismal sermon preached by their good friend Jim Limburg, in which he compared the psalmist's image to the knitting of a Norwegian sweater, which I take it is a very complicated creative enterprise. (I assume the sermon was preached in Minnesota and not in South Carolina and that the congregation understood the point.) And then Jim said, "If it is complicated to knit a Norwegian sweater, how much more complicated must it be to knit a Norwegian!"

However complicated it may be, each of us has been knit and woven into our being by the creative and loving power of God. Before our life, we were known to God; our days written in God's book before there was a single one of them. Each of us has been known, created, seen by God before we were even conceived. There is no way we can lay that out in any scientific or literal picture. Only the heart that belongs to God can know it is true.

The psalmist then says these words that let us know our whither is as known and as secure as our whence, that we are the Lord's after as well as before.

> How weighty to me are your thoughts, O God!
>   How vast is the sum of them!
> I try to count them—they are more than the sand;
>   I come to the end—I am still with you. (Ps 139:17–18)

In these words, the psalmist gives voice to the Christian confidence that the one who has said from the beginning: "I am with you always," says also to us at the end: "You are always with me." What matters in all this—and I believe it to be true with all my heart—is the Christian conviction, confirmed in the resurrection of Jesus Christ, that we are forever kept in the mercy and love of God. That was true before we were born; that will be true after we have died and our bodies have disappeared. Who and what we are still lives with God and is kept by God. And God will complete the work begun in us. Elsewhere the psalmist puts it—and I know this word primarily because my mother repeated it every day during the twenty years she lived after my father's death, "Precious in the sight of the Lord, is the death of his saints" (Ps 116:15).

Christians are often reluctant to say much about *heaven*. Maybe because any speaking of heaven runs too easily and quickly into images of pearly gates and streets of gold. Don would say heaven is more about an open door that no one can shut. I would lift up three things about heaven that resound from the Scriptures:

One is that the Christian hope of heaven is the conviction that *our final destiny is in God's care*—and that really is all we *need* to know.

A second is that heaven is already present to us in that cloud of witnesses that surrounds us this day and always. All those who have gone before encompass and keep us and bear witness to us beyond their life. And whatever we have known of loving relationship is not lost. How we shall experience that relationship beyond our death, we do not know. But it belongs to whatever future with God we have.

And the final thing to remember about heaven is this. I do not know what heaven looks like, but I know what it sounds like. Heaven is where there is—everywhere and nothing but—*the joy of music and singing*. When the Psalter comes to an end in Psalm 150 with the call of everything and every one to the praise of God, every instrument to play and every voice to sing hallelujah! it gives us a true foretaste of heaven and the communion of saints—who are surely clothed in choir robes. Even at the end—especially at the end!—we are still with the Lord, held forever by the everlasting arms, standing in that great chorus of witnesses that sings unendingly—and always in parts!—"Hallelujah, the LORD God omnipotent reigns!" And the amens go on forever.

I cannot prove this, of course, but I do not believe that we are misled by the gospel and the church's experience. Christian hope is not desperate. It is trusting and reliable, which means that we can take what comes in this world knowing that the God who is with us now will keep us forever and make our lives full.

One final word. Toward the end of his essay on Christian hope, Don Juel quotes the words of our Lord over the bread—"Take, this is my body"—and wine—"This is my blood of the covenant poured out for many"—at the table with his disciples, and particularly Jesus's words, "Truly, I tell you, I will never again drink of the fruit of the vine until that day when I drink it new in the kingdom of God." Then Don says this: "The claim that God refuses to accept death as the final word is made in light of a history of divine activity centered in God's raising the crucified Jesus from the dead. Crucial is how that reality becomes effective through the medium of human systems of signs that address particular people in their particular settings." (I take it he spoke proleptically at that point and meant this family at this time, this community, these friends.) "In the worship of the church," Don goes on to say, "where the risen Christ is present in the spoken word and in the sacraments, generations of Christians have testified that God gives birth to hope against hope."[3]

So now at this moment, gathered around the Lord's table, we bear witness to the truth of his words, testifying to one another and to the world, in company with all those who have gone before and are gathered with us even now at the table, that the promises of God are sure and can be trusted: Whether we live or whether we die, we are the Lord's.

3. Juel, "Christian Hope," 182.

Communion and Other Occasions

Taste and See

Old Testament Lesson: Psalm 34:1–10
New Testament Lesson: John 13:1–20

THE LESSON I READ from the Gospel of John deals with the preparation of disciples of Christ for communion and so is appropriate for our receptive hearing. These words also go beyond preparation to speak of the meaning of the supper at the Lord's Table and what it represents for the Christian life when the host at the table is gone. The Gospel does all that, remarkably enough, without really focusing on the supper itself. There are no words concerning the bread and the wine as in the other Gospels. Instead our attention is drawn to an act of Jesus that is not mentioned in Matthew, Mark, or Luke. It seems to be for the Gospel of John the crucial point of that last evening. I believe there are several dimensions of the account that are capable both of keeping us from misunderstanding and of helping us to understand properly the event we celebrate this morning.

To begin, the gospel will not let us fail to see who is really at work in the unfolding events or to turn our eyes from the fact that the path Jesus walked was one of obedience and not happenstance or fate. Twice we are told that Jesus knew what lay ahead of him and what it meant. He is not simply caught up in the stream of history. Events do not just run their course for Jesus. Lying behind them is the agency of God. The hour at hand is not just the hour of Jesus's death. It is the time for the working of the purpose of God. The one into whose hands the Father gives all things goes to his destiny agonizingly—as we know from Gethsemane—but also freely, knowingly, and by choice because his will and the will of God are one. John as much as any of the Gospels enables us to see that the person who is at the center of this drama is not simply a great person, a martyr who, as many others have done, demonstrates a higher way even at the cost of his life—a Sir Thomas More, a Dietrich Bonhoeffer, or the like. No, there is something more here, says John. What happens to Jesus and what he does is the activity and purpose of God. Lest we should think that it is only a Nazarene carpenter who falls before the onslaughts of human pride, hostility, and betrayal, these words in John 13 confirm what we already hear at the beginning of the Gospel, that God is fully present in Jesus's destiny. It is of cosmic significance.

That we might see the events associated with Jesus's death with blinded eyes and less than full comprehension is demonstrated all too well in the conversation between Jesus and Peter as the Master washes Peter's feet. It shows us once more—as has happened over and over again—how the most ardent follower can completely misunderstand the Lord he or she would follow.

Peter would take second place to no one in absolute devotion to Jesus—he who before that night was over would deny his master three times. Yet his very devotion obscured the words and deeds Jesus wanted him to hear and understand. Peter would have been a marvelous founder of a Jesus cult. His attitude over and over betrays his desire to see Jesus as a superior being above and different from all others, object of veneration, manifesting himself in exaltation. The one who is master and lord surely has no business taking the part of a menial servant! So when Jesus girds himself in a towel and takes the role of a slave to wash the feet of the disciples, Peter protests vigorously. At least he cannot be faulted for romanticizing footwashing. He knew it was an unpleasant, menial job and was aghast that the master would literally stoop to such a task. When the hero worshiper Peter protests and will not allow his Lord to wash his feet, Jesus reproves him and says that unless he washes Peter, he has no part in him. Whereupon Peter misunderstands once more in his ardent desire to be president of the Jesus fan club and asks for a full bath, shampoo, massage, the works. If washing does the trick and gets him in with Jesus, then by all means let's do the job right!

I do not underscore Peter's reactions simply for the sake of castigating him with the benefit of hindsight. The Gospel writer told this story because Peter was so representative of those whose discipleship would be more like the worship of the emperor than the worship of God, whose understanding of the majesty of God revealed in Jesus Christ is a majesty and glory of

kings and emperors and gods, when in fact as this story of the preparation for the Last Supper makes clear, that majesty is manifest in lowliness,
humiliation, and death; that power is a power made perfect in weakness.

The Gospel of John has much to say about the glory of God and God
being glorified in Jesus. But the clue to God's *glory* is very much in this story
and its aftermath of betrayal, denial, scourging, and death. In Lewis Car-
roll's *Through the Looking Glass* or *Alice in Wonderland*, Alice and Humpty
Dumpty have a conversation about birthdays in which Humpty Dumpty
points out that in a year there are 364 unbirthdays.

Then he says, "And there's only one for birthday presents you know.
There's glory for you."

To which Alice replies: "I don't know what you mean by 'glory.'"

"Of course you don't—till I tell you," says Humpty Dumpty. "I meant
'there's a nice knock-down argument for you.'"

"But glory doesn't mean a nice knock-down argument," Alice objects.

"When I use a word," Humpty Dumpty says scornfully, "it means just
what I choose it to mean—neither more nor less."

There is a quite profound sense in which that is just what happens in
the passion of Jesus—glory is redefined by God, who in effect says glory
means what I say it means, and now you see my glory manifest in the agony
and death of Jesus at the hands of a sinful and cruel humanity. One of the
many anomalies of Christian faith and practice—in this case a quite un-
happy anomaly—is that the cross and the crucifix have become objects of
veneration in churches and chapels, turned into silver and gold as if we
could turn the lowliness of the crucified God once again into our notions
of glory and majesty, when what it is really about is washing dirty feet and
the painful death of the innocent for the sake of others.

Peter misunderstood altogether. As far as I can tell, he did that every time. But his misunderstanding is capable of becoming a word to us, a
guard against our misunderstanding, against our attempt to gather in this
sanctuary to perpetuate the cult of Jesus and venerate him, when in fact
our gathering is in order to know again the experience of cleansing and
forgiveness and to see in Jesus's death the pattern of obedience that belongs
to the discipleship he seeks, that is, to taste and see the goodness of God.

The meaning of Jesus's death is at least that it was *an enactment* and *a
testimony to the forgiving love of God*. Through the crucifixion of Jesus, God
demonstrated and accomplished that word of cleansing and forgiveness.
Whatever else it was, it was no less than that. How that happened in Jesus's

death, how many were made whole and clean through his innocent death we are not told, and it remains a mystery beyond our fathoming though many have thought to grasp how it was accomplished. But to partake of the bread and the wine is to remember and celebrate and experience once again the reality of that love that makes us whole and clean. The psalmist in the depths of despair cries out: "If you, O LORD, should mark iniquities, Lord who could stand?" and answers his own cry: "But there is forgiveness with you . . . With the Lord there is steadfast love, and . . . great power to redeem" (Ps 130:3, 4, 7). "Taste and see that the LORD is good" (Ps 34:8).

Indeed taste and see the bread and wine that mark the goodness of God, a goodness that stands over against all the suffering and tragedy and evil and wickedness that mark and mar human existence. For that too is the meaning of the death of Jesus we remember on this occasion as we eat the bread and drink the wine. That strange willingness on the part of one who is the transcendent ground of all that is to take into God's own self the pain and suffering of the human lot. That is indeed scandal and foolishness—except for those who have also experienced the pain and suffering. For Jesus represents and stands with all of them in his death even as he represents and stands with God in saying No to all of that. "This is my body which is broken for you"—and for all broken bodies and minds. "Taste and see."

There is one more word that must be said lest with Peter we fail to perceive what it is the Lord does as he girds the towel about him and washes the feet of his disciples. "If I your Lord and Teacher have washed your feet, you also ought to wash one another's feet. For I have set you an example, that you also should do as I have done to you." All this footwashing stuff, the clothing of the slave, which is what the knotted towel is all about, is his way for us. But it is also our way for others. This is no slave mentality, though it is sometimes confused with that. Jesus's word to slaves was: "You are free." This is not a call to those whose lives are confined to menial service of others to see that service into which they are forced as obedience to Jesus Christ. Perhaps there are ways in which that can be said, but I doubt it and not very easily in any event. That is not the call of Christ here. Rather, it is his command to those who know and affirm their own worth, who are not forced into servitude of any sort, those disciples of Christ in the First Presbyterian Church of Lansing or the Nassau Presbyterian Church in Princeton—people of status and wealth and power—to relinquish their power and let their status go in the surprising service of others who, like

Peter, do not expect such loving service; to become members of what one person has called with reference to this story "the guild of the knotted towel," the "union" of those laborers whose service of Christ is manifest in the service of others.

So "Taste and see." Know in this moment as you eat the bread and drink the wine that you have been cleansed, and go and wash the feet of others. "For I have set you an example, that you also should do as I have done to you."

What Does God Do about Sin?

Old Testament Lesson: Genesis 50:15–21

New Testament Lesson: John 21:15–19

THERE WAS A TIME when the subject of sin was uppermost in the preaching of the church, and in some places and some preaching it still is. One has only to recall the vivid pictures of Jimmy Swaggart tearfully confessing his sins and asking for forgiveness from the Lord, his family, and everybody else. But in Presbyterian pulpits and congregations such heavy focus on sin is much less the case. Many of us find that we are repulsed by a lot of talk about sin—indeed even at the image of Swaggart confessing his before all the world. We dislike it and feel browbeaten when we are preached at a lot about sin. Periodically I will hear someone raise a question about a worship service that always begins with a confession of sin in which we declare in various ways how bad we are.

There are probably a variety of reasons why we have these feelings about sin. It may be because we genuinely do not see ourselves as constantly beset by sin if sin is, as the Catechism says: "Any want of conformity unto or transgression of the law of God."

Also, we have come to a broader understanding of human activity that affects our understanding of sin. Some of the sins that in past times have been denounced so vigorously seem to many now trivial or not even morally questionable: for example, card playing, dancing, and even such things as drinking, gambling, profanity, as well as some kinds of sexual activity that have been traditionally regarded as sinful. We know also that much of our behavior is affected by psychological, hereditary, and environmental factors that are not easily controlled by the will to do good. What we have often in the past called sin and wickedness can be seen in some instances now to look more like sickness and the pathological.

Our difficulty with the notion of sin is also created by the fact that many of us carry such a heavy load of guilt and shame about ourselves and our life already that for the church and its preaching to focus heavily upon that is simply to increase an already intolerable burden. We are aware of our failures as husband, wife, parent, sister, citizen, and neighbor. We know of our corporate sins of indifference, neglect, and injustice. We even are well aware that we participate in larger dimensions of corporate guilt: being a part of a society that in various ways, to which we contribute whether we intend to or not, oppresses and harms others by racial attitudes, by affluence gained at the expense of others and not easily shared with those without it, by lack of attention to human need. I am constantly reminded of that in everything I see around me and constantly trying to ward it off.

Yet with all that being true, one still has to ask if it is not the case that ignoring this dimension of our experience may have some negative effects. In doing so, we may be ignoring, covering over, suppressing or failing to come to terms with the moral dimension of our lives, with the various pulls within us toward self-centeredness and self-idolatry, or even neglect of self or of others. We may also find that some sicknesses or maladies of the soul are not subject to the usual therapies of even the best doctors, psychiatrists, analysts, or psychologists.

And I, no more than anyone else, can offer miracle therapies, or super healing balm for those individual and corporate burdens of guilt that all of us carry in some form or another. I do believe that the reality of sin and guilt and shame, whatever shape they or it may take, is experienced in relationship both to those other people whose lives we touch and to the God who undergirds our lives and shapes the destinies of all of us. Further, most of us, I think, want somehow for that problem to be dealt with. And among those pieces of good news proclaimed in the Christian gospel is the sure word that God is present in and through our individual lives and our common history to deal with the offenses and wrongs we have committed.

I want briefly to remind you of three stories in the Bible that show some of the ways that God deals with the wrongs that human beings carry out. They by no means exhaust the possibilities of the divine mercy or God's power to release us from the burden, but they can give us some clues to carry with us, pointers to God's graciousness.

The first of these stories is the familiar account of the paralytic brought to Jesus who was lowered from the roof because the crowd was so great. What stands out in that story is not so much Jesus's healing of the sick man so that a paralyzed man could walk, but that his primary concern was to declare to the crippled man the forgiveness of sins. Now while this declaration may reflect a seemingly easy association of sickness with sin, the story cannot be let go very easily. It reminds us that the therapy that really heals may have at its very center the word of God's forgiveness. This is the first story in the gospel that makes clear what the *whole* story is all about, that God's freeing and forgiving love is demonstrated and achieved in the life and ministry, the death and resurrection, of Jesus Christ. He was and is God's word of forgiveness. Then and now those touched by him in any way can find a release, the realization that in the most ultimate sense those wrongs we have done are not held against us, that the slate is always being wiped clean, that we may experience in the fullest sense a freedom from sin and guilt. I have some ambivalence about the necessity of a confession of sin at the beginning of every worship service, but I am convinced that no more crucial and important word is ever uttered from this pulpit than the words—and the reality to which they point—"I declare unto you in the name of Jesus: Your sins are forgiven."

Another story, this time from the Old Testament, also tells about what God does about sin, but in a somewhat different way than the forgiving word that Jesus announced in the gospel and declared to the paralyzed man. It is the story of Joseph, which I trust is familiar to most of you. At the conclusion of the Joseph story there is a final episode that uncovers what that story is really about. The death of their father, Jacob, arouses in the minds and hearts of the brothers the fear that now that Daddy is dead, Joseph may finally pay us back for the wrong we did to him years ago. So they go to him and ask him not to turn their sin against him back against them but to forgive their jealous and harmful actions.

Joseph's response is an interesting one. He sees in their approach a view that the matter of how their offence will be dealt with is entirely in his hands, that he is in effect being seen as in the place of God when in fact he is not. What the brothers do not realize is that God has already dealt with this sin. It has been dealt with not so much by forgiveness as by the providence of God. *The brothers* intended harm and did so. That was part of the reality of Joseph's life. Yet somehow in the mystery of God's purpose *God* was intending something good and did so. And that too was a part of the reality of Joseph's life. How these two things—the brothers' harm and God's good—can all be a part of the same act the story does not say. There is indeed a mystery here that we cannot easily penetrate, and the story does not encourage us to try to explain the ins and outs of God's providence or to assume in an overly simple way that God always turns human sin into good. The Bible does not tell us that. But here it does tell us a very important story about the conflicts among some brothers that results in the brothers trying to do in one of their number. That is wrong; there is no way of getting around it. But their story is part of a much larger story of God's care for people, in which the brothers' offense becomes a part of the way in which God provides for the larger community. Joseph does not actually forgive the brothers' sin against him; nor does he turn it back on them in revenge now that he has power. Rather he perceives that God has dealt with it providentially and his task now is neither to forgive nor to avenge, but to provide, to be the instrument of God's good purpose that overcomes and subsumes the human wrong.

There is one more story I shall mention that also gives an answer to the question posed in the title of the sermon. It is the account at the end of John of Jesus's appearance to some of the disciples after the resurrection. Peter is the key figure in the story. *He* suggests that they go fishing. *He* is the one who jumps into the water to swim to his Lord when he sees him and then goes to the boat to haul out the fish when Jesus asks for some. Then after breakfast Jesus and Peter have a conversation in which Jesus asks Peter the same question three times and follows it with a command. Now to understand that conversation one must remember that among those persons close to Jesus whose culpability or participation in the crime against Jesus is the greatest, Peter, along with Judas, stands to the fore. How will Jesus deal with Peter's denial of him, at one and the same time an offense against his Lord and an all too natural or human act of fear and cowardice? Well, the story tells us. The sin against his Lord must be dealt with, but this time Jesus does not simply say to Peter, Your sin is forgiven. Several other things happen, however. As with Joseph's brothers, there is no condemnation here on Jesus's part. We have no record here that Jesus reproved Peter for his denial. But the denial of the past is turned into a new confession of trust and loyalty. Matching Peter's denial three times, Jesus three times puts to him the question: "Simon, do you love me?" And three times Peter vigorously replies: "Yes, Lord, you know that I love you." The denial is replaced by a new affirmation of faith. The refusal to acknowledge Jesus is transformed into an enthusiastic devotion. And even further, Peter's failure, his offense against his Lord is not met by reminders of his denial, warnings not to do it again, not by words of reproof or requirements of penance, but by a gracious renewal of faith and a call to vocation, to the service of the one Peter had earlier denied.

Here again, therefore, God deals with the human offense not so much by forgiveness. Rather through the words of the risen Lord, God takes the one who had sinned and turns him into a faithful servant. Calling to vocation and discipleship are the outcome that God brings from the human act.

I have placed before you these stories, Jesus's healing of the paralyzed man, Joseph and his brothers, and Jesus's final meeting with Peter—to try to illustrate the variety of possibilities within God's purposes in dealing with even the negative parts of our life and action. We cannot neatly determine at every point how God will respond to our misdeeds, our individual and corporate failures to live and act according to our own and God's intentions. What we can do is open ourselves to the manifold and gracious ways that God can overcome or transform our offenses and wrongs, our sins— through the forgiving grace that is found in Jesus Christ and experienced over and over again in our human relationships; the possibilities of God's accomplishing God's good out of our wrong even if we do not always see that good, as Joseph's brothers did not; the experience of renewed calling to vocation and service rather than condemnation and penance. I hope, for example, out of those manifold ways that we as a people or nation sin against our sisters and brothers, often not even knowing how or seeing the results of our actions and policies, that God, out of a gracious providence, will work out a larger good for humankind. And, to be specific again, is it not possible in the face of the sense of wrong and guilt in the broken relationships of marriage and family that God may be calling us not to live under divine condemnation or self-condemnation but to renew our sense of vocation to the Lord?

So these are the three stories and a word they have to say to you. I realize I have not told you a list of things to go out and do. But, then, this sermon, like many of the stories of the Bible is not about what *you* are to do but about what *God* has already done and will do, about the gift of release from guilt and new possibilities for life. And that, I believe, is why the gospel really is a piece of very good news.

The Glory of God and Human Glory

Scripture Lesson: Psalm 8

THE QUESTION OF WHO and what we are as human beings and what is our place in this universe of time and space is one of the issues that not only arises in the mind of each of us but is a central concern of Christian faith. There are various ways that the Christian tradition has given answer to that question, conversing with but also challenging other views. This morning I want to suggest that the eighth psalm is one of those voices in Scripture presenting a perspective on the human situation that is basic to the Judaeo-Christian tradition and worthy of our attention even if it is sharply different from some of the other dominant ideologies of our time.

It would be a mistake, however, to begin by assuming that this familiar psalm has as its *primary* intention to offer theological reflection on human nature. Its fundamental aim is both to express as well as to call forth from the worshiping congregation the praise of the God of creation. It is about human glory (and we shall come to that), but it is human glory under and derived from the glory of God. If there is any doubt about that, one has only to note how the song begins and ends—with the same jubilant shout of praise: "O LORD, our Lord, how majestic is thy name in all the earth!" (Ps 8:1). The community of ancient Israel saw in its daily life, in the blessings of a prosperous land, in the victories and defeats of its armies, in all these things, the work of God; but over and over again it found the grandest testimony to the rule of God and the majesty of God in the created order, a universe of such vastness, complexity, power, and beauty that by its very existence it renders praise to the one who in mysterious power has brought it into being, always guiding and ordering it. The psalmist looks at the heavens, the moon and the stars, and is overwhelmed to see this magnificent work of the fingers of God.

And here is one of the places where the passage of time and the onset of modernity have done little to modify the reaction of the psalmist. I doubt if there is anyone here who has not at some time stood in the night as did the psalmist and gazed in awe at the skies, looking at a beam of light from a star and realizing that beam has been traveling 186,000 miles per second toward us for millions of years. And in the very silent wonder, our beings, often inarticulately, praise the Creator of it all.

Several years ago when my family was spending some time in England, our youngest son, Patrick, came home one afternoon from a long visit with his school friend Martin. Mary Ann and I realized very quickly that something was clearly troubling Patrick greatly. When we asked him what the problem was, he said, "I don't think that I can tell you." We became very concerned at that point, wondering what in the world had happened at the friend's house. Finally we pressed him into telling us. With great reluctance he confessed that he had discovered that his friend did not believe in God. That certainly was not what we had imagined, and we breathed a silent sigh of relief as we asked him what he had said to Martin upon discovering this devastating fact. He replied, "I asked him how he thought the earth and the planets and the stars got here if there is no God."

Patrick's response was naïve and expressed a way of thinking about God that even some theologians would reject. But I think there is an element in the midst of that naiveté that is undeniably on target. Not as if one could read a doctrine of God out of the created order or give solid proof of the existence of God. Attempt that and it will probably provoke as many problems as it resolves. Rather it is to see in the mysteries and wonders of the universe some of those clues, those rumors of angels, as Peter Berger calls them, that point us to the majesty of God; and to hear in the music of the spheres the praise of the God that made them and whose glory transcends them all.

So the psalm in its basic affirmation expresses and bids us out of our own wonder and awe to join in praise of the Maker of heaven and earth.

But if it begins and ends in that praise of God, at its center, the psalm is focused upon the human creature. For the psalmist's gaze upon the universe has produced *two* reactions: one is a spontaneous reaction of praise; the other is an equally spontaneous and even more inevitable question. It is the question about the place of human beings in such a vast universe:

When I look at your heavens, the work of your fingers,
  the moon and the stars which you have established,
what are human beings that you are mindful of them,
  and mortals that you pay attention to such (Ps 8:3–4).

It is a very obvious question, and the answer seems equally obvious. But before turning to it, let me place alongside the question and the thoughts of this stargazer of many centuries past the thoughts and words of a contemporary stargazer. He is Stephen Weinberg, a physicist and astrophysicist who has written a fascinating book titled *The First Three Minutes*, and subtitled *A Modern View of the Origin of the Universe*. In the book, he seeks to present for the intelligent layperson a picture of what is the general if not unanimous consensus of contemporary science about the beginnings of the universe. He suggests approximately when the universe began, describes what the initial explosion may have been like, and then, in some detail creates a sort of movie scenario of the first three minutes of the universe's history. At the end of the book he speculates about the future, whether the universe will go on indefinitely expanding or fall back upon itself in a return to its original beginning point. Then he concludes with these words:

> However all these problems may be resolved, and whichever cosmological model proves correct, there is not much of comfort in any of this. It is almost irresistible for humans to believe that we have some special relation to the universe, that human life is not just a more-or-less farcical outcome of a chain of accidents reaching back to the first three minutes, but that we were somehow built in from the beginning. As I write this I happen to be in an airplane at 30,000 feet, flying over Wyoming en route home from San Francisco to Boston. Below the earth looks very soft and comfortable—fluffy clouds here and there, snow turning pink as the sun sets, roads stretching straight across the country from one town to another. It is very hard to realize that this all is just a tiny part of an overwhelmingly hostile universe. It is even harder to realize that this present universe has evolved from an unspeakably unfamiliar early condition, and faces a future extinction of endless cold or intolerable heat. The more the universe seems comprehensible, the more it also seems pointless.
>
> But if there is no solace in the fruits of our research, there is at least some consolation in the research itself. Men and women are not content to comfort themselves with tales of gods and giants, or to confine their thoughts to the daily affairs of life; they also build

telescopes and satellites and accelerators, and sit at their desks for endless hours working out the meaning of the data they gather. The effort to understand the universe is one of the very few things that lifts human life a little above the level of farce, and gives it some of the grace of tragedy.[1]

Weinberg's gazing at the stars produces for him an answer to the kind of question that erupts from the mouth of the psalmist, an answer that would seem to be the direction toward which the psalmist from a religious rather than a scientific view is moving. We are "just a tiny part of an overwhelmingly hostile universe" that becomes more pointless the more it is comprehensible. Only a very few things "lift human life a little above the level of farce." More surprising than such a conclusion on the part of Weinberg is, I think, the conclusion of the one who speaks through the psalm, one who sees no less clearly the vastness of the cosmos and knows its threatening potential. Over against a judgment that human life is a "little above the level of farce" comes the claim that the human is little less than divine. The grandeur of the universe and the transcendence of God lead not to a view that human beings are puny bits of matter inexplicably set in a tiny corner of a hostile universe, but that they are like God. They are kings in the kingdom that is God's universe, both in their nature—crowned with glory and honor—and in their purpose—to rule the works of God. Not by accident but by the loving intention of God who has made us "little less than gods," who has crowned us, given us rule over that very universe that seems to render us mere specks of cosmic dust.

Now, my friends, if one is looking for a high anthropology, an optimistic view of human life, I think one can go no further than that. While other voices sound in the pages of Scripture, this understanding reverberates from beginning to end. You cannot get past the first page of the Bible—let me put it another way: you are *not supposed* to get past the first page—without discovering that such a view of human nature and purpose is the initial assumption of God's story with and for humanity from beginning to end. That is, of course, a claim of faith. One may as well reject it as claim it. Not all the evidence leads to such a conclusion; I shall come back to that. But two things need to be emphasized: First is that it is fundamental to the Christian view of our life under God that God has given to women and men a divine nature, a royal purpose, a central place in the cosmos. Second, it makes all the difference in the world if this is

1. Weinberg, *The First Three Minutes*, 154–55.

your starting point—the conviction of the worth and grandeur of human creation, of a man or a woman, that is given by God. To set such a view as your starting point, your basic assumption, greatly affects how you think and work and act.

I know a psychiatrist who seems to me to have a rather naïve distaste for talk about sin and the devil and tends to reject such out of hand. But she has marvelous healing results with people with all sorts of problems that many of the rest of us would regard as belonging at least in part to the realm of sin and the devil. I think that her success is due in part at least to her deep conviction that every one she sees is first and fundamentally a child of God and so to be viewed and treated. What I am suggesting is that much of what we believe and do in life grows out of our basic assumption and starting point about the human condition and that one of the strongest notes in Scripture is this view of human being as reflecting the nature and rule of God.

We cannot leave the psalm without realizing, however, that in and out of Scripture another answer altogether is given to the question about humankind that comes forth from the psalmist. That question is repeated two more times in the Old Testament. In the 144th Psalm (vv. 3–4):

> O LORD, what are human beings that you regard them,
>   or mortals that you think of them.
> humankind is like a breath,
>   whose days are like a passing shadow.

And in Job (7:16ff.):

> I loathe my life; I would not live forever.
>   let me alone for my days are a breath.
> What is a man that you make so much of him,
>   that you set your mind upon him,
>   visit him every morning, test him every evening.
> . . .
> Let me alone that I may swallow my spit.

Here is a very different attitude, where the sense of a special place in the creation has become a man's burden and God's attention not a sign of God's grace but a part of his affliction.

These words have been called a parody of Psalm 8. But that is to belittle both Job and his words, which reflect his sense from his own terrible experience of a tension between the religious tradition that claims a special place in the creation for each of us as persons and life as it is often actually lived. Further, there are many who would find Job's words more true to their experience than those of the psalmist. For there *is* a dark side to human experience in the reality of suffering, tragedy, and inhumanity—a dark side that cannot be glossed over or eliminated either from reality or from our vision.

I read about it yesterday in the newspaper in the continuing story of the violent death of a black man in Howard Beach and the report of a county thirty miles north of my hometown of Atlanta in which no black person has dared to set foot for seventy-five years. I saw it the other night on television in a film clip of a new and very authentic movie about Vietnam that showed a soldier with a pistol placed against the head of a small girl, and I remembered other such pictures of executions in the streets of Vietnamese cities and young children screaming and naked with their clothes burned off by napalm. And as I thought about these things yesterday I remembered the inexplicable death at Christmastime of the little child of a couple at the Seminary and wondered how many other children died last night of the ravages of disease and hunger. But I knew that I did not really want to know.

When all that presses upon me, it becomes clearer to me why the author of the Letter to the Hebrews applied the words of Psalm 8 to Jesus and his experience, seeing in his suffering and death the crown of glory and honor. Psalm 8 holds good. Even in the face of the threats and tragedy of life, it is not merely an idea or wishful thinking. It describes God's intention for us and our place in God's creation. It remains the basic assumption we hold about ourselves and every other person. But in the good news that is declared and demonstrated in the life, death, and resurrection of Jesus of Nazareth, another word comes into our midst, confirming that indeed God has given to us as human beings a high place in all God's creation—and even more. The extent to which God is mindful of us and pays attention to us, as the psalmist says, is only fully seen in the love that is manifest in Jesus Christ, who is God's identification with humankind in its glory *and in all its suffering and tragedy and shame.* The latter cannot be denied as a part of our human fate. It can and has been taken up into the fate and the heart of the very God who made and crowned us.

There is much that remains yet unseen to me in all of this. It is capable of theological reflection and discussion, but not I think susceptible to easy resolution and understanding. But what matters is sufficiently clear and comprehensible to me in a photograph that I saw several years ago enlarged on the walls of Norwich Cathedral in England. It was a picture of a Catholic nun bent over feeding a truly skeletal figure of a man so starved or wasted with disease that he had only about 12 hours of life left, according to the caption below the photograph. Nothing in all that beautiful cathedral is now more vivid in my memory than that picture of an unnamed sister in her flowing white robe holding the head of her dying and even more anonymous brother as she fed him. I truly believe that in that act she crowned him with glory and honor even as she demonstrated the love of the one she follows, that in the midst of the evil and suffering of human life God pays attention and God cares.

Amen, and to God be all the glory.

The Things That Make for Peace

Old Testament Lesson: Psalm 122

New Testament Lesson: Luke 19:41–44

Tomorrow we come to the table, as Jesus and his disciples did on the night of his betrayal. Before we do, there is a bit of unfinished business I think we need to tend to. It has to do with Jerusalem. Last Sunday, the lection that many of us heard or preached was Luke's account of Jesus's triumphal entry into the city with cloaks spread on the road before him, people praising God and saying: "Blessed is the king who comes in the name of the Lord. Peace on heaven, and glory in the highest heaven." We may not have noticed that in Luke, unlike Matthew and Mark, there is no triumphal entry. There is a big parade, and we learn eventually that Jesus is in the temple when we hear of him raising hell chasing all the religious salesmen out of the house of God. But the glorious entry into the city is stopped short with the text that I just read:

> And when he drew near and saw the city, he wept over it, saying,
> "Would that even today you knew the things that make for peace!
> But now they are hid from your eyes."

Before his personal anguished lament from the cross, Jesus laments for the world. As our eyes are focused in this week on Jesus, his own eyes are focused on the city and its failure to recognize the things that belong to its peace. I would suggest that on our own journey to the cross, we take note of what brought forth his tears and listen to his lament over the city.

If ever there is a moment when the Christian church is inclined to turn completely in on itself, it is in this week. Surely, that is okay. The story of Christ's passion, death, and resurrection is the great story, the one that brought the church into being, that brought *us* into being. But Lent and Easter week are very much a looking inward; the journey to the cross is a walk that Jesus had to take, and we must not look away from it—except that *he* did. Before the agony of the cross, his own tears were for the city (not for himself), the city that did not know the things that make for peace.

Jesus only wept twice, I believe, once for a friend who had died and once for the city that could not recognize wherein lay its peace. I presume that his tears, like our own, are clues to the things that matter most. If so, the things that make for peace matter most, the peace of the city, the peace of Jerusalem.

What do we do with Jerusalem? That question has always been with us. We have handled it in various ways whether in this text or in any text. We can historicize it as we remember the destruction of Jerusalem in AD 70 and so take care of Jesus's tears that way. Oh, that's what he was talking about! So having put the text in its historical framework, one that, of course, is long past, we can go on to Gethsemane and Golgotha.

Or we can interpret Jerusalem in all sorts of other ways, as the church has classically done in its multiple senses of Scripture: the literal city of the Jews, the tropological human soul, the allegorical church, and the anagogical heavenly city for which we hope. All of these things Jerusalem surely represents. Even as all of these interpretations are ways to escape the reality of what Jerusalem is. It is a city of Jews and Arabs and so is not finally our concern. It is the heavenly city, so we can read Jerusalem that way and leave the reality of the Jerusalem we read about each day in the papers as one more contemporary political problem.

But to do so is to forget that, whether we like it or not, by theological heritage and by contemporary reality, Jerusalem is our city. We have our own roadmap for it and for its peace. A lot of people want to live there. Some people have to live there. Some people can't live there. Some people are dying, literally, to go there. I'm scared to go there. So pray for the peace of Jerusalem.

Jesus's words over Jerusalem stand in a powerful continuity and an equally powerful tension with those words of the psalmist. "Pray for the peace of Jerusalem," we read. And so Jesus does, for he knew the psalms well. But his is hardly the psalmist's prayer "Peace be within your walls, and security within your towers." It is a cry of despair, a wish for the impossible: "Would that you, even you, could know the things that make for peace. But now they are hid from your eyes and your guard towers and high walls will not bring *shalom*."

We must read the Gospel text carefully, however. There is not a word about Jerusalem in it. "As he came near and saw *the city*, he wept over it . . ." Of course, it is Jerusalem. But Jerusalem in the biblical texts and reality is always more than that. Its peace and conflict always reflect a larger or broader struggle within the human community to learn the things that make for peace.

So whether the city is Jerusalem or New York or Baghdad or Washington, or Falluja, or wherever, Jesus still weeps for the city that does not know the things that make for peace, and we who live in the city have to ask if they are forever hidden from our eyes.

Maybe they are, but if that is the case then I think we have not fully heard the rest of this story that began outside the city walls in Jesus's lament. The Easter affirmation is that he is our peace. In this one who wept over the city and suffered for it lies our true peace. There can be no equivocation about that meaning of the gospel. Not in other messiahs, not in utopian dreams or in grandiose political visions but in his way in the world with us and through us.

It is not enough, however, to say our peace is found in him. That is the most important thing to say. But if that is all we say and do and stop, then we are guilty of theological platitudes and have defaulted in our responsibility as theologians and disciples. Perhaps the things that make for peace are still hidden from our eyes. But in his steps and in his way, we are impelled to seek them out. So I am going to make a start on the list and let you continue it as you leave this place:

1. War does not make for peace. If you think that is a plea for pacifism as a philosophy, then I am not being clear. I am simply stating a fact: War is not among the things that make for peace. War is violence and destruction. War is bodies dead and mutilated, cities blown up, and always overwhelming grief. War does not make for peace.

2. Telling the truth makes for peace. In our common life and in our political life, honest discourse about the way things are, what we are doing, and how we can do better is one of those things that can make the city flourish and prosper.

3. Keeping the Commandments makes for peace. The closest parallel to Jesus's lament elsewhere in Scripture is found in the book of Isaiah: "Oh that you had paid attention to my commandments! Then your prosperity [your *shalom*] would have been like a river . . ." To live

by the commandments is to do at least two things: One, to put our ultimate trust in God and thus free ourselves to risk what it takes to pursue the things that make for peace; and two, to set our face resolutely toward our neighbor and her well-being, remembering that if Jesus were to tell his story now, the man beaten and left for dead in the ditch would be an Israeli and the one who stopped to help him a Palestinian. We are still trying to find out who is our neighbor.

4. Peace and prosperity and human flourishing arise in the city when its leaders and rulers—as Psalm 72 so vividly reminds us—"have pity on the weak . . . deliver the needy when they call, the poor and those who have no helper." Until we learn to govern that way, there will be no peace.

5. Finally, the things that make for peace will always have to come by way of Jerusalem. Whether its contemporary inhabitants, visitors, and neighbors like it or not—whether we like it or not—Jerusalem is and always has been a paradigm, a special place, the human city seeking to be the city of God. If religious groups and ethnic groups cannot live together in harmony there, then there is probably little hope for any of the rest of us. If a rule of law that is torah-shaped gives way to a rule of law that is oppressive, then can the human community find any law that truly works for and effects justice? Whether it is living with neighbors that is at issue or welcoming the stranger, or creating an environment where, in the words of the prophet Zechariah, "Old men and old women shall again sit in the streets of Jerusalem, each with staff in hand because of their great age. And the streets of the city shall be full of boys and girls, playing in its streets" (Zech 8:4), Jerusalem is at the moment—and perhaps always—a test case for the viability of the biblical way in this world.

So, pray for the peace of Jerusalem. That is not a common Christian prayer. But then we have not always placed either Jerusalem's well-being or prayer very high on the list of things that make for peace. This psalm and Jesus's tears bid us do that, pray for Jerusalem and seek its good.

You probably noticed that I have left the most difficult and hardest words of this text untouched. Frankly, I am not sure what to say about them. Anything I can think of serves only to ease them out of the way. So here at the end, I will simply read them once more and let you deal with them:

Indeed, the days will come upon you, when your enemies will set up ramparts around you and surround you, and hem you in on every side. They will crush you to the ground, you and your children within you, and they will not leave within you one stone upon another; because you did not recognize the time of your visitation.

So Jesus said, as he wept.

Love the Stranger

Old Testament Lesson: Deuteronomy 10:12–22

New Testament Lesson: Matthew 25:31–40

THE BRITISH NOVELIST C. P. Snow is probably best known for his nine-volume story of Lewis Eliot—lawyer, Cambridge professor, and civil servant. While each novel has its individual title, Snow gave to the whole work the rubric *Strangers and Brothers*. I do not know if he ever commented about that title as a way of viewing the series as a whole, but I discern in it an awareness of a rather basic fact about human relationships: simply that we encounter other persons for the most part either as brother/sister or as stranger. On the one hand, we live with and relate to people as friends, neighbors, kinfolk, those who belong to the family or the community, however narrowly or broadly we may define that. These are our brothers and sisters. But we also run up against people, or they come to us, as persons we do not know, as strangers, with whom we share no bonds, or commitments, no common contexts or experiences, no presuppositions that we have anything in common.

Our instinctive reaction to each of these categories and to people who fit within them is very different. The image of brother or sister and the reality embodied in sisters and brothers is generally a positive one. That doesn't mean that some of us may not have lousy family relatives, but we know from our experience what brother and sister love is. We depend upon that and build our primary relationships, if not our primary meaning in life, on a network of those kinds of relationships, that is, with members of our family or our church, with good friends, with people with whom we work closely.

Our reaction to the stranger, whether the actual stranger or the thought of the stranger, is quite different. We approach that category with uncertainty, questions, hesitation, and often alarm—all the more in these recent months. The very term *stranger* is a rather ominous one. Look at any book title or movie title with that word in it, and you will see what I mean: *A Stranger Is Watching, Strangers on a Train, When a Stranger Comes.* The stranger is the outsider we do not know, and precisely because we do not know her, she may in various ways threaten our well being and certainly has no claim upon us in the way that sister and friend do.

What is clear from the Bible, however, is that the stranger no less than the sister/brother is a *moral* category, one whose very existence in our midst requires of us certain modes of action. Indeed in a most fundamental way the moral obligation that falls upon us in the face of either brother/ neighbor or stranger is the same. Our text from Deuteronomy is very direct about that with its simple imperative: Love the stranger.

The laws of the Old Testament—which is where we hear most about strangers—were not unclear about how such love for brother or stranger was manifest. It was less an attitude or emotion, though it may include that, than it was a structured system of respect, care, protection from harm, and provision for life. The love of neighbor never sits in Scripture simply as a nebulous good feeling. It takes shape in particular, ongoing, predictable, and obligatory acts in behalf of the well-being of the neighbor. And so it was and is meant to be with the stranger who comes to us.

But there is more to it than that, and I believe we need to probe a little further to hear what is at stake in the various biblical instructions about strangers. I want to lift up for specific focus three aspects or implications of the biblical injunction to love the stranger:

1. First, we need to keep in mind that when the Bible speaks of the stranger, or the sojourner—which is often the term used in the translations—it has something quite specific in mind with reference both to the *who* and the *what*, to the one who is the stranger and to the act that demonstrates love. The term *sojourner* uncovers more clearly who the stranger is. The stranger is not the hostile figure encountered in a blind alley or on a transcontinental plane who threatens our lives and against whom one takes proper precautions. In some contemporary translations, the word for *stranger* is translated as "resident alien." Some have translated it, with equal accuracy, as the "transient" or "immigrant." The stranger, you see, is the resident alien, the immigrant, the transient, who comes into our midst, who comes from outside our circle, however that may be defined—another place, another country—into our world without the network of relationships that

can be counted upon to ensure care, protection, and acceptance—the one who belongs to another group, another country, but now is at my door, in my school, working in the office next to me, maybe living down the street from me.

And loving the stranger, according to Scripture, has a particular kind of action that is its identifying mark. It is the act of *welcome, of hospitality*, of taking the outsider into our circle. Some years ago, when Mary Ann's parents and some of their brothers and sisters were visiting in our home, Mary Ann placed a tape recorder in their midst as they told stories of their childhood in Kentucky. I was struck, as would be anyone who listens to that tape, by how many of the incidents and stories that were recalled with laughter and joy were occasions of simple and automatic acts of hospitality. They told about how when they grew up on the farm, people used to come through the country looking for work, transient, migrant workers. One of them was Uncle "Pomp" Baxter, just a drifter who showed up every spring. One of the sisters says on the tape, "He liked to do just whatever there was to do, and we would take him in the house." Another who would come by from time to time was Iz Brennegar. He had a rather unusual vocation. He trapped polecats (skunks), they said. For obvious reasons, they could always tell when he was coming toward the house. And again, one of the children, now eighty years old, remembered: "Father always used to welcome him"—and with a pause as she slowly recalled what she had never noticed as a child—"like he did everyone who came to the house."

No single action defines such hospitality and welcome, but there is one act that has come to symbolize it in Scripture and often represents true hospitality to the stranger in life. That is the *sharing of a meal*, a simple act that, more than any other in our ordinary experience, provides for human needs, builds friendship, and makes us feel at home. No meal takes place without human energy and labor. All shared meals have the potential to build intimacy and community. The sharing of a meal or a feast is a frequent event in Scripture and a primary image for all God's good gifts to humankind. What is particularly noticeable is the inclusiveness of the meal, whatever the occasion. Deuteronomy specifically makes the point that even the stranger is included in the celebrative feasts of the family and the community. Precisely there where all the good gifts of God are celebrated and enjoyed is where there is a place at the table for the stranger, the resident alien, in our midst. The Scriptures specifically and often remind us that the immigrant among us is to share in our good blessing, in our prosperity, which is not by the power of our own hands but by the power and blessing of God.

2. A second feature of the biblical injunction to love the stranger is the fact *that in welcoming the stranger we discover surprising possibilities and wonderful happenings.* That is what we hear in Jesus's parable of the great judgment when the astonished folk who are gathered around the throne of the King wonder when they met him as a stranger and welcomed him, only to hear that it was as they met the stranger at their door, that they showed hospitality to the one who is their Lord. The writer of the Letter to the Hebrews says the same thing in a different way: "Do not neglect to show hospitality to strangers, for thereby some have entertained angels unawares" (13:2). Various biblical stories tell of such surprising possibilities in the welcome to the stranger, from Abraham's gracious hosting of three men who come by his way (and later in the story turn out to be messengers from God) to the journey of two disheartened disciples on the Emmaus road after the death of Jesus who meet a stranger and offer him food and lodging at the end of the day, only to discover that they have welcomed the Risen Lord to their house and table. So we hear of the possibility that in our hospitality to the stranger, we may be extending an unintended and indeed unrealized welcome to the one who has welcomed us.

But there is a clue here to something else, and that is the fact that in entertaining strangers we experience the wonder and surprise of discovering others, their worlds, and their stories. So as I listened to the tape of Mary Ann's family telling their childhood stories, I heard them tell of their laughter and giggles as these unusual and different people broke into their world with a different style of life and unconscious humor, and I remembered my own childhood during the Second World War when our house seemed always to have servicemen and -women visiting and gathered around the table Sunday after church. I remembered Kenny Barber, who taught me how to shoot a pistol, and Major Chu, a Chinese officer who turned out to be a poet and wrote me a poem that I carried around in my small billfold until it disintegrated and disappeared. It was about gossamer wings. I never hear the word *gossamer* that I do not think of Major Chu, who first taught it to me in a sensitive, beautiful poem.

3. The final thing to be said, then, is at one and the same time an inference of all that I have said and its ground. It is simply this: *Our experience of the gracious welcome of God frees us and opens us up to love the stranger, so that the demand becomes a gift and the chore becomes an opportunity.* "Love the stranger," the Bible says, "*for you were strangers in Egypt.*" Those who know what it is to have been alien people seeking welcome and hospitality find themselves drawn to the welcome of others.

For the Christian community the reality that we have been welcomed as strangers is the perpetual invitation to come to the table where the Lord is host. It is truly a sign and seal that we have been "taken in." Once you have been welcomed and made at home you know what that is like. What is God's way with us becomes our way with others. Perhaps this word can best be made clear by the account of a small incident that a friend told in the following way to Roy Fairchild, a teacher at San Francisco Theological Seminary:

> I had come to Vienna after a two week illness in a little Austrian village. I had spent most of my travel money on medicine and doctors and used my last bit to take a train to Vienna. I had no clue as to where I could find my friends who had been waiting for me earlier. I was lost and hungry and depressed. As I was standing in one of the streetcar stations in the center of the city, tired, discouraged, and trying to figure out what to do, a little, old wrinkled woman (whose job it was to sweep out the station) came over to me and asked if I was hungry. Even before I could answer, she took her lunch from a brown bag and offered me half. I was moved. She not only helped my aching hunger, but lifted my spirit in an unforgettable way. I have never forgotten her—the warmth of her face, the graciousness of her gift, the youthful sparkle in her eyes. We talked for more than an hour about her life. It had not been easy. She was raised in the country, knowing nothing but hard work on a farm. She had lost her husband and two sons in the Resistance. Only her daughter had survived. But she was thankful, she said, for many things. She was at peace with her story. Finally, I asked her why she offered me her lunch. She said simply, "Jesu ist mein Herr. Gott ist gut." [Jesus is my Lord. God is good]. She understood and lived the story of Jesus in the way that the most sophisticated scholars could never do. Her faith touched mine. Who was it, after all, that I met that day in Vienna.[1]

1. Fairchild, *Finding Hope Again*, 136.

Unless the Lord Build the House

Old Testament Lesson: Psalm 127

New Testament Lesson: Ephesians 4:4–7, 11–12

ABOUT THREE YEARS AGO, Mary Ann and I built a house, or rather had a new house built for us. We had never done that before and learned a lot in the process. One of the results of that experience is a realization that it is not as easy as I thought it would be to say *who* built our house. It was a complex process, effected by many persons, elements, and influences. During that time, we often told our friends we were building a house. That is true, but not quite true, or at least much too simple a way to put it, as any of you who have built a house are well aware. We initiated the project, provided the land, contracted with persons, expressed our desires. We had definite ideas about what it should be like. We are paying for the house (with the considerable help of a bank, without which we could not build the house). The size and problems of the site, however, made it imperative to get the help of an architect, and during the planning stages it was increasingly our sense that the *architect* was building the house more than we were. It clearly reflects and depends upon his vision and his abilities. But of course, none of the persons mentioned so far actually built the house. It was finally built by an able contractor of some forty years, whose skill and integrity and training of other workmen, who in fact actually built the house, were the final determiner of the success of the house and the extent to which it works and accomplishes the purpose for which it was created.

I trust that the connection of all this to the 127th Psalm is in some fashion obvious if indirect. Certainly the experience I have been describing has made me sharply aware that the matter of *how human structures are built* and *by whom* is quite complex, that they are created by the involvement of many agents, the skills and directions and visions of various persons. The good accomplishment of such enterprises is dependent upon the immediate skills and effort of those who put hammer and saw to wood, who set concrete, who install pipe and electrical wire. But without good plans and the vision of the house by architect and contractor, the structure would finally be banal or inefficient or at worse a disaster that doesn't stay up or won't last.

It is out of such human experiences that the imagery of Psalm 127 is drawn. It speaks in its opening verses of *house* and *city*. It does not stop, there, however, for it goes on to speak of daily work and of the family, as if to say to hearers and readers of this psalm that *every* human endeavor is doomed to vanity without the Lord's involvement and direction. All our large enterprises are faced with the prospect of emptiness, of no good and useful purpose finally coming forth from the human energies and actions invested therein apart from the direction and shaping that is wrought by the hand of the Lord.

The four specific examples of human activity and structures mentioned in the psalm—house, city, work, and family—are significant in themselves. It is no accident that this psalm is ascribed to Solomon, the master builder of cities as well as of the house of the Lord, the temple. That heading at the beginning, "Of Solomon," suggests that it is for such leaders and builders of God's house and of human communities that this psalm has been written. The house that God builds can be many things. It was and continues to be first and foremost the sanctuary where the congregation gathers before God. The *house* referred to in this psalm is the representation of God's building of the community of faith and its material, political, and spiritual structures. It is the household of faith, the church, that comes to life by the power of God at work within it but is empty and pretentious when it exists for its own end and knows not who its master builder is.

"Unless the LORD watches over the city, the sentry stays awake in vain" (Ps 127:1). The city is here the representation of God's building and of keeping/protecting the community of people, the political and social communities embodied in our cities and towns, in our nation, in those communities that are the context for the everyday living of life in a secular world that is, in reality everywhere touched by the finger of God. The words of this psalm are a profound challenge to those of us who claim as our motto, "In God we trust," and who pledge allegiance to "one nation under God." Is this in fact a political community whose builder and maker is God, one whose character is shaped by the prophetic calls for mercy and righteousness and the care of society's least, by Moses's exhortation to love the Lord your God and keep the right commandments of God, by Jesus's call to seek first God's kingdom and God's righteousness? The psalm is an abrasive counter also to any of us who regard our towns, cities, and nation as human structures that exist or can exist *apart* from the power and guidance and care of the Lord. At our best we have known that the city or nation, as much as the church, endures and ensures blessing and peace, justice and righteousness, only as it is kept and directed by God's instruction.

That has been said as directly by some of our political leaders as it has been by the church. The opening verse of this psalm was the closing sentence of the speech President Kennedy was to have delivered on that fateful Friday in Dallas when he was cut down by an assassin's bullet.

It was also to the opening verses of this psalm that Benjamin Franklin, hardly a religious divine, appealed when speaking before the Convention assembled to frame a Constitution for the United States of America:

> All of us who were engaged in the struggle [with Britain] must have observed frequent instances of a superintending Providence. To that kind Providence we owe this opportunity of consulting in peace on the means of establishing our future national felicity. And have we now forgotten this powerful Friend? or do we imagine that we no longer need His assistance? . . . if a sparrow cannot fall to the ground without His notice, is it probable that an empire can rise without His aid? We have been assured, Sir, in the sacred writings that 'Except the Lord build the house, they labour in vain that build it.' I firmly believe this, and I also believe that without His concurring aid we shall proceed in this political building no better than the builders of Babel. I therefore beg leave to move that, henceforth, prayers imploring the assistance of Heaven and its blessing on our deliberations, be held in this assembly every morning before we proceed to business . . .[1]

A third sphere of human activity appears in the psalm that is before us; *work, human labor*, is here the representation and symbol of God's provision of what we need for our individual existence:

> It is in vain that you rise up early
>   and go late to rest,
> eating the bread of anxious toil;

The psalm places a negative judgment on the approach to life that centers in constant driving of oneself in laborious, anxious, hard work. It

---

1. Prothero, *The Psalms in Human Life*, 175.

claims that such a way of going about the human enterprise of work is as useless, vain, empty, and without effect as seeking to build a house or secure a city without God's active involvement. It is a part of our ethos as Protestants, as Americans, to value work very highly, to identify ourselves by our job or profession, to exalt those who work hard and long, to believe that the problem of poverty is solved by putting everybody to work.

The Bible is not so enthusiastic about work. To be sure there are condemnations of laziness in the Proverbs and elsewhere. But this psalm gives two very important qualifications about human labor. One is the basic point of the psalm, that any human work or labor to create the structures of life and provide for them, is useless without God's effective participation grounding or undergirding that work. And second, hard or anxious toil defined here as a frantic, racing, ceaseless involvement in work is useless, period, because God is the one who gives prosperity, honor, and rest. We might find that hard to believe, that it is not finally our driven efforts but God's gift that sustains us, but I think it would be worth our trusting. It would affect the lives of many of us profoundly in terms of what we expect of and give to our families, what the congregation expects of its pastor, what it expects of its members. Here is a note of grace, one that offers us a possibility of release from the drivenness of our lives if we can believe it and act upon it by letting go the frantic pace of our work.

The last of the human endeavors is the creation and raising of a family. "Lo, children are a heritage from God." The psalm reminds us of the truth we know well, that children can be one of the richest manifestations of the blessing of God on human life and one of the clearest points where people sense the mystery and joy of God's gift. Here also, however, one is not likely to enjoy children and family *as blessing* unless the "house," the household, that is built in and through them is built by and under the Lord.

We cannot finally avoid, of course, the question of how it is that God builds the house, watches over the city, gives honor and rest to those who labor and blessing through the gift of children. Any attempt to answer that question must do so modestly, for it is one thing to believe that God's involvement in our life and work is a necessity for their fulfillment and their good, and it is another thing to claim to know the mystery of God's ways with us.

Indeed it is just that point that must be made, lest we claim too much too quickly. God's involvement in our activities, God's providential sustaining and establishing of the work of our hands is in the truest sense a mystery, a wonder that happens and often surprises us with joy, that, as Franklin realized, we sense only in retrospect; but is not like the kind of invisible ink I once had as a boy, that if you just rub some theological lemon juice on it, all will become visible, that the ways of God's work among us to build the church and watch over our political communities will be self-evident and obvious. To trust that God will build the house does not mean we know how. If my architectural image at the beginning gives us any clues, it suggests that God's ways of building the house will be complex and not easily discernible to those who pass by.

Yet one can say just as surely and straightforwardly that we do know something of how God will be at work in our building and keeping of church and city, of family and workplace: In the act of teaching our children the ways of the Lord—the love of sister and brother, moral uprightness toward the neighbor, trust and obedience to the one who made us and calls us to be God's people; in God's gift and call of some to be pastors and teachers, to equip the saints for the work of ministry, for *building up the body of Christ*; in the selection of leaders of our religious and political communities according to the biblical criteria, articulated by Moses and reaffirmed by the prophets—women and men who are wise, discerning, compassionate, courageous, and full of integrity; in carrying out our jobs, our various daily responsibilities, in ways that make life more human and in full awareness that, as Deuteronomy says, God is the one who gives us the power and the gifts to obtain the goods of life.

When those who build the human structure of church and nation, of city and family, of work and wealth, are instructed by the word of God, when they know—when *we* know—what Jesus claimed his Sadducean challengers did not know—the Scriptures and the power of God—when we are shaped and directed in every sphere of life by a vision of the kingdom of God and seek that kingdom and God's will in every endeavor, then the Lord will truly build the house, and our labors will not be in vain.

Keep These Words in Your Heart

Old Testament Lesson: Deuteronomy 6:4–9, 20–25
New Testament Lesson: 2 Timothy 1:1–7

THE BOOK OF DEUTERONOMY is one long Sunday School lesson, in fact a little longer than most of us would tolerate unless we could spread it out over several Sundays. One of the things that is noticeable when you read or study that biblical book is its large concern for *teaching the children*, for instructing the next generation. What the people learn from Moses and the Lord, they are to pass on to the children and the grandchildren and the great-grandchildren, so that each new generation shall be prepared to stand before God and to "fear the LORD your God."

How, then, does education that leads to a life lived in the fear of the Lord take place, and what is its substance? There are some clues from our text that help us out at this point. One thing that is said over and over is that the faith and its implications for life are to be *the subject of constant attention and discussion*. In the text I read from Deuteronomy, the scene is of a family, of parents and children, in continuing and lively conversation about the meaning of their experience with God and God's expectations of them. Explicit teaching by the parents to the children, conversation about the faith and its implications—whether around an issue or problem that has come up or in relation to the worship service and the sermon that was heard that morning, or whatever—reflection on God's instruction for our life is an ongoing enterprise in the family and the community. Deuteronomy suggests, and this was meant as practical wisdom for family life, that whether at home or away from home, the most important things of the faith—and they were embodied especially in the command to love the Lord your God with everything that you are and have, and to love your neighbor as yourself: those most important matters are to be uppermost in mind and heart, called to mind first thing when one gets up and recalled as one goes to sleep each night. One of the things that the prayer at bedtime does for the child is to instill in her or him an awareness at the end of the day of what it means to be a child of God, to be held in loving hands and called to a faithful obedience—even as a child or a young person.

The educational process in Deuteronomy is also often *a response to the questions of the child or young person* as a means of explicating our relationship to God. Teaching the faith is not only something we try to build into the family system and into congregational life. It is something that will happen quite ad hoc and spontaneously as the questions arise. The children's questions are always there: "What is that?" "Why?" "Why do I?" ("What does God look like?"). Such questions become the impetus for teaching the next generation the meaning of the rules and regulations we follow: Why do I have to do what you tell me? Why is it wrong to tell a white lie? They become the impetus for interpreting the social and religious practices we keep (why do we have to go to church every Sunday?), and for explaining the signs and symbols of the faith (why do we eat that little piece of bread and drink that small cup of wine in the church service?). In the hand that places water upon a child's head, in the act of breaking and eating bread, of pouring and drinking wine, we embody and enact the faith. At the same time we evoke questions about what we are doing that become an occasion for saying more about body and blood inexplicably but gracefully broken and shed in our behalf to say to us, "You are forgiven; and I am with you. You don't have to be afraid in this fearful world."

What is particularly interesting about the way the Scriptures depict the response of the parent or teacher to the religious question of a child is that the answer to the question often is not a rational or theological answer but a *story*: "When your children ask you in time to come, 'What is the meaning of the decrees and the statutes and the ordinances that the LORD our God has commanded you?' then you shall say to your children, 'We were Pharaoh's slaves in Egypt, but the LORD brought us out of Egypt with a mighty hand'" (Deut 6:20–21). There is probably no more powerful way to convey meaning than by story. And we live by the stories. There are probably few persons here who could give much detail of what is in the Constitution of the United States. Yet all of us are powerfully committed to it. And that is because we know its story, and its story is our story, the story of a people's struggle to be free and to live in ways of justice and equity and freedom. We are so shaped by that story that we commit ourselves to the directions and ideals embodied in the constitutional document without even having to know what they are. We know the *story* of the struggle for freedom and independence, for the right of worship and free speech out of which the Constitution came.

So as a parent, a teacher, a grandparent or someone else tells the story, the one who hears, child or adult, finds in the story of God's way with us, with our fathers and mothers long ago, indications for how we are to live now. What happens is that the telling of the story serves to *create a memory* for the new generation, for those who were not there and do not know: We were Pharaoh's slaves in Egypt, and the Lord brought us out and freed us to be God's people in the world. So here is how we now live as God's folk in the world. We were there when they crucified our Lord, and God raised him up from the dead, so we need never be afraid of death again.

That leads me finally, then, to ask *why* we teach and learn and keep these words of faith, of liturgy and Scripture, of catechism and theology, of family story and faith story in our hearts. There are two reasons that I shall just mention. There are other reasons, but these are enough. One is simply to *help us deal with the questions of meaning in life.* The question of the child in our text is, literally, "What are the statutes and ordinances?" But the translation properly says, "What do the statutes and ordinances *mean?*" The questions we ask when we are young are followed by yet more questions as we grow old, as we encounter the contingencies and uncertainties of life. The child's question, where do I come from? is still there when we grow older, but now at a deeper level: it becomes the question about our whence and our whither, about what is happening in the world, about what it all means or whether there is any meaning to it all. Christian faith lays claims to some thoughts about those matters, some answers to those questions. They are couched in mystery but not in darkness and ignorance. Those of us who are older learn the faith to teach the young; and those who are younger learn the faith for when they grow older.

And that leads me to the second reason for keeping these words on your heart. They are there to *help us make it along the way.* My guess is that there are probably three texts from Scripture that most of us learn when we are young if we do not learn anything else. They are the Lord's Prayer, the Ten Commandments, and the 23rd Psalm. Why is that? Why these texts? It is not difficult to discern why. the Lord's Prayer so that we know how to pray to God. If we have no other words to say (whether we are grateful or scared to death), here are some that will do in any and every circumstance. The Ten Commandments to give us direction for our lives. They may not be all we need to know, but their observance will carry us well along the way. And we learn the 23rd Psalm when we are young so that we have it when we die, so that a familiar text, learned by rote, can become our story when all is said and done.

When I was a child, I learned the Shorter Catechism. I cannot remember hardly a single question and answer now except the first one, which asks, what is our chief end in life? Many of you know the answer as well as I, even if you did not learn the catechism. It is to glorify God and to enjoy him forever. Also when I was young, our mother made us children learn the 103rd Psalm: "Bless the LORD, O my soul, and forget not all his benefits, who forgives all your iniquities, who heals all your diseases, who redeems your life from destruction, who crowns you with steadfast love and mercy, who satisfies you with good as long as you live . . ." There are many more verses. We had to learn them. I had to learn them again when my sister insisted that we all recite that psalm at her wedding. Why did my mother have us do that? I know now of course: Because those were the words that we turned to when my father died and then when she died. My friends, the first question of the Westminster Shorter Catechism and the 103rd Psalm can carry you all the way to the end. You don't need much more than that.

The book of Proverbs speaks about the teaching and instruction of a mother and father in the same way that our text from Deuteronomy does about the Great Commandment, but it adds something quite important. It says, "Bind them upon your heart always; tie them around your neck. When you walk, *they will lead you*; when you lie down, *they will watch over you*; when you awake, *they will talk with you*." We keep these words of Scripture and faith in our hearts finally because *they* will *keep us*; they will lead us, however long and difficult the journey, all the way to the end.

A Last Meal

Old Testament Scripture: Isaiah 25:6–9

New Testament Scripture: John 13:1–20

IN HIS BOOK *On Being a Christian*, the Catholic theologian Hans Küng titles his discussion of the meaning of the Lord's Supper not with any of the expected terms: the Mass, the Eucharist, communion, and the like, but simply "A Last Meal." I am appropriating his phrase as the rubric for this occasion, that we may think and act, pray, and eat in awareness that what we do in this hour is both to share a last meal together and to celebrate the last meal that Jesus ate with those he loved.

We have spent a number of years together. Some a short while; others for three, four, fifteen, twenty years, or more. And we know that in many ways we shall be in contact with each other as the years go by. But the reality is that, after today, we shall not sit at table together again as we have done in various ways through these years. Many of us will be leaving, and others will be coming to take our place. I expect that those of us who are leaving are more conscious of this than those who remain. And if that be sentiment, so be it. I have no fear of or distaste for sentiment. More important, I am convinced that it is instinctively, theologically, and humanly right that our last meal together should be the one we share with our Lord.

So with particular attention to the Gospel of John as it tells us of that last evening of Jesus with his disciples, I want us to think and hear again what it means to partake of the Lord's Supper as our last meal together.

THE GOSPEL

What is heard first and most clearly and more important than anything else is the *gospel*, the good news of the love of God for us in Jesus Christ. (I hope that either consciously or subconsciously whenever you take up a text for its proclamation you ask, how is that God's good news?) I think that good news comes to us in many ways. But surely it is not said any more simply or clearly than in the opening words of the chapter I read a few minutes ago: "Now before the festival of the Passover, Jesus knew that his hour had come to depart from this world and go to the Father. Having loved his own who were in the world, he loved them to the end."

"He loved them to the end." There is the gospel. It is as simple as that. But it says much about the quality and extent of that divine love that was incarnate in Jesus of Nazareth. He loved them to the end; that is, literally to the very last breath of his human life Jesus loved his own, his very death being a final act of love for us. "To the end," that is, utterly, totally, without reserve; to the end and beyond which it is not possible to love, giving totally of himself even unto death out of love for us. And "to the end" in yet another sense when we know that this is a word about us as those whom Jesus loved to the end. It is to the end of *our* lives, too, that Jesus's love encompasses us and marks our destiny forever. I think that is the most important thing I can say to you this morning at our last meal together: Wherever you go, whatever the years ahead may hold for you, you are loved utterly and unceasingly.

What the Evangelist recounts so simply at the beginning, Jesus then exemplifies during the meal as a symbolic act demonstrating and pointing to this love to the end. Jesus puts aside his outer robe, wraps a towel around his waist like a servant, and proceeds to wash the feet of the disciples. The familiarity of the episode should not blind us to its apparent absurdity, an absurdity grasped immediately by Peter who protests the action. What is the one who is Lord doing in the role of a slave or servant? The one who stands in their midst as the agent of God, indeed God's own dear Child, humbles himself to become a servant tending to their needs. Peter sees nothing but the overt act, which makes no sense to him. He does not want the Lord to do this menial act for him—until it is necessary. Then he thinks he must need a whole bath! In both responses, he shows a natural reaction, on the one hand (v. 8) an unwillingness or inability to see the salvation of God wrought out in such lowly fashion or the presence of God in the form of a slave; and on the other (vv. 9–10) the refusal to see the uniqueness of the salvation gift, that it is not a matter of more or less, but a once-for-all gift that accomplishes God's purpose.

Jesus realizes that Peter and the disciples cannot fully comprehend his action until after his passion. It is from this side of the cross that we can see the knotted towel and the footwashing as an act representing the meaning of the death of Christ. It has a double meaning as it symbolizes Jesus's death. It is a way of pointing to his humiliation in death, the scandal of the cross, and the power of God wrought out of weakness and powerlessness. But such humiliation unto death is in behalf of those whose feet are washed. They are cleansed by his death. The act of the slave sets them free. The one to whom all is given (v. 3) gives it all away in behalf of those who have nothing. And we now sit at table with the other disciples as those whose feet are washed, whose sins are forgiven through his humiliation and death, who at this table know as surely as we ever shall that we are loved to the end.

The Call to Service

There is, of course, another meaning that Jesus gives to his act: "Do you know what I have done to you? You call me Teacher and Lord—and you are right, for that is what I am. So if I, your Lord and Teacher, have washed your feet, you also ought to wash one another's feet. For I have set you an example" (v. 14). The last meal together and with Jesus, therefore, not only reminds us afresh of that love that holds us fast, but it also sets the shape of our ministry in the world. That ministry is a ministry of humility and service after the example of Christ. It is not forced upon us. Nor should we take up such a ministry as an ascetic burden. We are called to it by the deed and word of Jesus. To take willingly the role that we do not already have—that of becoming a servant, freely and by choice. It is not an action expected of one by the definition of others, only by the definition of Christ.

I doubt that any word of Jesus is more important for those of us who assume his ministry—whether in large church or small, youth ministry or seminary teaching, mission work or whatever. Our ministry is one of humility and service, the washing of one another's feet. But remember—that is an act of love. And by such loving acts shall the Christian community live out its existence. "As I have loved you . . . you also love one another." That means *because* Jesus has loved us beyond imagining, to the end, and *in the manner* of his love—self-giving even unto death.

Past, Present, and Future at the Last Meal

Finally, I want to say that not only do we hear and see in this meal together the gospel of God's unreserved love for us in Jesus Christ and its consequent call to a ministry of loving service in his name. The occasion also serves to take our theology of the sacraments out of the textbooks on systematic theology and out of the ordination exams and place it in the very particular and very human context of our life together—past, present, and future. For this day and this service is filled with memories for us: two, three, four years of study or more; years of teaching, fellowship, worship, ministry in various ways to one another and to others. Pain and anxiety, joy and pleasure. All these are part of our memory this morning and part of why we gather together here. But at the center and transcending all those other memories as a reason for our being here is the memory of our Lord's death. It is to remember again and afresh that love to the end that we come to the table.

Yet there are hopes as well as memories that we bring and take from the table. Hopes about marriage, new fields of ministry, children just arrived and yet to come, new homes, further study. All of these are there in our midst. Yet at the center and above all these lesser hopes, this last meal sets our minds and hearts on that fulfillment of God's purpose when all shall sit at banquet together and death shall be swallowed up forever, and the Lord God will wipe away all the tears from our faces. So in this meal our life is set between memory and hope. And what ties them together in the present is the presence of our Lord. It is what we experience here as we eat and drink. It is what undergirds us as we go from here.

So there you see is what I think the last meal means for us. But a caveat at the end. The truth is that it is not finally a last meal for us. For we shall eat this meal with our Lord and each other often. Wherever the name of Jesus is found and manifest, wherever the service of Jesus is carried out by those who through his death and his example belong to the guild of the knotted towel, there we shall sit down together at the Lord's Table wherever we are, in remembrance and hope, sustained by the presence of him who loved his own to the end and who calls us in turn to love and serve him to the end.

Our Life in Praise of God[1]

Old Testament Lesson: Psalm 136:1–9, 26

New Testament Lesson: Ephesians 1:3–14

WHILE IT DOES NOT happen much any more, some of you who are my age and older may remember learning as a child or a young person the Westminster Shorter Catechism. It was published in a small pink tract form. I learned the answers to all 107 questions and would have been absolutely aghast if I had known at the time that there was in fact a larger version of the same thing that was 200 questions and three times as long!

Virtually all of that memorization is now gone from an ever-aging brain. But there is one question and answer that remain forever in my memory. And many of you who learned and forgot the Catechism and even some of you who never learned it will also know the question and the answer. It is one of the most important questions in the Presbyterian and Reformed tradition, the first question of the Shorter Catechism, which asks simply "What is the chief end of man?" What is our chief purpose and goal as human beings? The answer is as simple as the question: to glorify and to enjoy God forever. That question and its answer set the theme of this sermon: that doxology is our reason for being and joy the final outcome of God's way with us. The goal of human life is to live in thanksgiving and praise of God. Or as the Letter to the Ephesians puts it, we have been destined to live for the praise of God's glory.

In the Bible where hymns and songs of thanksgiving abound, especially in the Psalms, there is a kind of simple logic to how praise happens. The hymn begins with a declaration or call to praise: "I will extol you, my God and King"; or hallelujah, "Praise the LORD." And that call to praise is

---

1. Part of this sermon is drawn from the author's essay "In Praise and Thanksgiving," *Theology Today* 45 (1988) 180–88; reprinted in Miller, *Theology Today*, 114–23. Used by permission of Westminster John Knox Press.

then grounded in a reason for praise, an indication of what God has done that evokes such a response. Something has happened—recovery from sickness, the birth of a child, the restoration of a relationship between parent and child, the realization of peace where there was hostility—where these are real and the hand of God is felt in their accomplishment, the only way to deal with that is in praise and thanksgiving.

The verse that opens the 136th Psalm and then becomes the repeated refrain is a typical example of the way that praise and thanksgiving work: a call to praise and thanksgiving ("O give thanks to the LORD") and then a reason, in fact two of them in this case ("for the LORD is good; for God's steadfast love endures forever"). This verse is not only a typical example. It became the model of praise in the Bible. We hear it again and again in the psalms, and when reference is made in other books to the people and the priest praising or giving thanks, it is these words they have in mind.

In this definitive hymn, the congregation declares—we declare!—our fundamental understanding of God in the reasons given for exalting and thanking God. To speak of God as good is to affirm that the Lord is the source of all that makes life possible and worthwhile, the deliverer of those in trouble and distress, the one who in making this whole universe marked it forever as "very good." To give thanks because God's steadfast love endures forever is to render joyous praise to God because we are forever supported and held by arms that are both loving and faithful, that in what matters most, our future is not at all unknown—we are kept by God's good for us, by God's enduring, unfailing love.

The purpose of praise becomes clear in this single verse: to respond to the experience of God's grace and power, to exalt the one who is seen and known to be that way, and to bear witness to all who hear that God is God and God is good.

Significant, sensible, and familiar as this call to praise God may be, it is not without its problems—for some at least. Some persons, I know, have experienced what C. S. Lewis has described in this way:

> When I first began to draw near to belief in God and even for some time after it had been given to me, I found a stumbling block in the demand so clamorously made by all religious people that we should "praise" God; still more in the suggestion that God himself demanded it. We all despise the man who demands continued assurance of his own virtue, intelligence or delightfulness; we despise still more the crowd of people round every dictator, every millionaire, every celebrity, who gratify that demand. Thus

a picture at once ludicrous and horrible, both of God and of His worshippers, threatened to appear in my mind. The Psalms were especially troublesome in this way—"Praise the Lord," "O praise the Lord with me," "Praise Him." (And why, incidentally, did praising God so often consist in telling other people to praise Him? Even in telling whales, snowstorms, etc., to go on doing what they would certainly do whether we told them or not?).[2]

I think Lewis may not be alone in such sentiments, and that may be why much praise of God is somber and unenthusiastic. What is expressed is duty and obligation when such notions seem to be totally counter to either praise or thanksgiving. The praises of Israel may help us in this regard. For the praise of God takes place two ways there. Much of the praise of the community arises out of concrete experience when one perceives the help and deliverance of God. Such praise is spontaneous, real, and enthusiastic; and where we find in our own experience the sense of the presence and the delivering help and the strong comfort of God, then our praise will be neither duty nor obligation; nor will it be seen as something required of us; it will be as real and natural as the praise of the Psalms.

On other occasions, Israel rendered more generally praise of the majesty and power and wonder of the God of creation, praising the Lord because God is god. Such praise may seem, or indeed be, more difficult on our part, but, as Lewis perceived, to acknowledge the glory of God in this way is analogous to acknowledging the beauty of a flower—simply because it is, and its beauty elicits from any and all beholders the exclamation of praise and wonder. And when one experiences that, praise is real, extravagant, and unavoidable. Indeed, the very enjoyment is not fully realized without the expression of praise and wonder.

Think of how it happens when you take a summer walk in the woods. As you are walking along, suddenly your eye spots a beautiful wildflower. You stop and exclaim, "Wow! Look at that! Isn't it beautiful!" One cannot avoid the exclamation of praise. It just happens because of the wonder of the flower's beauty. So it is with the praise of God.

Perhaps this is what the Shorter Catechism is after when it says that our chief end as human beings is to glorify and enjoy God forever. To enjoy God *is* to glorify God, even as lovers always glorify each other, whether for particular reasons or experiences or simply because of the relationship,

---

2. Lewis, *Reflections on the Psalms*, 90–91.

both always expecting the glory and praise of the other, but neither giving it only because it is expected.

Let me then make two claims about praise and why it is important in our life. The first is that *praise and doxology are among the most subversive things the church ever does.* For doxology to God undercuts all human structures and every human being as pretenders for ultimacy or absolute devotion. Praise places us totally outside ourselves except as gratitude for the good that has been done to and for us. Thanksgiving, whether to other persons or to God, is an inherent reminder that we are not autonomous and self-sufficient and by its very character directs our positive feelings toward others rather than toward ourselves. Praise to God does that in a kind of fundamental way as it directs our love away from self and toward God, not because we are unworthy but because the wonder of God's power and love and grace evokes our admiration and adoration, as when one hears the beauty of a symphony and is so caught by such beauty that all attention is directed toward the source of that wonder. In the hymn we shall shortly sing, Fred Pratt Green expresses this subversive character of praise:

> When in our music God is glorified
> and adoration leaves no room for pride,
> it is as though the whole creation cried, "Alleluia."[3]

Doxology, however, also serves to subvert the claims of any *other* person or structure to have ultimate place in our lives. It is the most visible regular expression of our obedience to the first commandment. Any community that sings with conviction: "All people that on earth do dwell, sing to the Lord with cheerful voice; Him serve with mirth, his praise forth tell"—cannot give its ultimate allegiance to any human group or person.

Which means also that the church's praise is one of its clearest testimonies to the reality of God in a world that either denies or is indifferent to the God who made it. Praise and prayer make no sense in a world where God is not present or trusted. The act of doxology is a continuing testimony to another order than the one that assumes we have found all the answers in ourselves and have no other way to go than the path our human minds and wills can identify.

My second and final claim about the praise of God is that it is *utterly useless—and that is the reason we do it.* The answer to the first Catechism question is a rather astonishing definition of the chief end of human life in

---

3. Green, "When in Our Music God is Glorified," *The Presbyterian Hymnal*, 264.

this world—to glorify God and enjoy God forever, as astonishing as those words in the letter to the Ephesians that say we "have been destined according to the purpose of him who accomplishes all things . . . so that we . . . might live for the praise of his glory" (1:11–12). Such words set aside all utilitarian goals, all efforts to identify moral purpose or worthwhile functions, and claim that our chief purpose in life is doxology and joy. In the face of a persistent and accepted pattern in our secular life *and our church life* that leads us always to live and work to accomplish things, to carry out goals, to live useful lives, and to set up unceasing lists of programs to justify our existence, the sound of doxology frees us to do nothing but give glory to God. The thing that matters most is completely useless in a world that measures activity by its usefulness, and human worth by capabilities and accomplishments, that asks us to identify ourselves to each other always by what we do.

And here is where music finds its place. Not its use, its place. The sound of praise is *music*. Praise and thanksgiving do not get their full expression apart from music. The stories and psalms of the Old Testament reverberate with the sounds of instruments and singing. As the Psalter reaches its end, it becomes nothing but doxology, and every instrument in the orchestra is called to play, every voice in the cosmic chorus to sing the praise of God.

It is interesting and somewhat strange, I think, how much the church worries about music and always seems to need to justify its place in worship and the church—and in the budget. Does this reflect reluctance to place at the center of the people's life that which has no other purpose than to glorify God? "Sing to the Lord a new song," is one of the most repeated lines in the Psalter. The *Shorter Catechism* suggests that is our reason for being. If that judgment is correct, then singing psalms and hymns of praise and playing the organ, the flute, and the trumpet are among the definitive acts of obedience. So let the music of Bach and Handel, of Thomas Tallis and Johannes Brahms, of John and Charles Wesley and Isaac Watts, of Black spirituals and Plainsong, of Ned Rorem and John Rutter ring in our churches. It will accomplish nothing. All it can do is express joy and give glory to God.

Bibliography

Barth, Karl. *Church Dogmatics*, I/1. Translated by G. T. Thomson. Edinburgh: T. & T. Clark, 1936.

Bergant, Dianne, with Richard Fragomeni. *Preaching the New Lectionary*. 3 vols. Collegeville, MN: Liturgical, 1999–2001.

Bonhoeffer, Dietrich. *Discipleship*. Translated by Barbara Green and Reinhard Krauss. Edited by Geffrey B. Kelly and John D. Godsey. Dietrich Bonhoeffer Works 4. Minneapolis: Fortress, 2001.

———. *Letters and Papers from Prison*. Edited by Eberhard Bethge. Translated by Reginald Fuller. Rev. ed. New York: Macmillan, 1967.

Bright, John. *The Kingdom of God: The Biblical Concept and Its Meaning for the Church*. Nashville: Abingdon-Cokesbury, 1953.

Brueggemann, Walter. "'Impossibility and Epistemology in the Faith Traditions of Abraham and Sarah (Genesis 18:1–15).'" In *The Psalms and the Life of Faith*, edited by Patrick D. Miller, 167–88. Minneapolis: Fortress, 1995.

———. *Theology of the Old Testament: Testimony, Dispute, Advocacy*. Minneapolis: Fortress, 1997.

Buechner, Frederick. *Wishful Thinking: A Theological ABC*. New York: Harper & Row, 1973.

Calvin, John. *John Calvin's Sermons on the Ten Commandments*. Edited and translated by Benjamin W. Farley. Grand Rapids: Baker, 1980.

———. *The Sermons of John Calvin upon the Fifth Book of Moses Called Deuteronomy*. London: Middleton, 1583.

Creach, Jerome F. D. *Yahweh as Refuge and the Editing of the Hebrew Psalter*. Journal for the Study of the Old Testament Supplement Series 217. Sheffield: Sheffield Academic, 1996.

Dahl, Nils. "The Neglected Factor in New Testament Theology." *Reflections* 73 (1975) 3–8.

Das, A. Andrew, and Frank J. Matera. *The Forgotten God: Perspectives on Biblical Theology*. Louisville: Westminster John Knox, 2002.

Dempsey, Carol J. *The Prophets: A Liberation-Critical Reading*. Liberation-Critical Reading of the Old Testament. Minneapolis: Fortress, 2000.

Dowey, Edward. "Law in Luther and Calvin." *Theology Today* 41 (1984) 146–53.

Ebeling, Gerhard. *Kirchengeschichte als Geschichte der Auslegung der Heiligen Schrift*. Sammlung gemeinverständlicher Vorträge und Schriften aus dem Gebiet der Theologie und Religionsgeschichte 189. Tübingen: Mohr/Siebeck, 1947.

Eliot, T. S. *The Complete Poems and Plays: 1909–1950*. New York: Harcourt, Brace & World, 1952.

Fairchild, Roy W. *Finding Hope Again: A Pastor's Guide to Counseling Depressed Persons*. San Francisco: Harper & Row, 1980.

Green, Fred Pratt. "When in Our Music God Is Glorified." In *The Presbyterian Hymnal*, no. 264. Louisville: Westminster John Knox, 1990 (Quoted with permission).

Jenson, Robert W. "The Bible and the Trinity." *Pro Ecclesia* 21 (2002) 329–39.

———. *Systematic Theology*. Vol. 1, *The Triune God*. Oxford: Oxford University Press, 1997.

Juel, Donald L. "Christian Hope and the Denial of Death: Encountering New Testament Eschatology." In *The End of the World and the Ends of God: Science and Theology on Eschatology*, edited by John Polkinghorne and Michael Welker, 171–83. Harrisburg, PA: Trinity, 2000.

———. *Messianic Exegesis: Christological Interpretation of the Old Testament in Early Christianity*. Philadelphia: Fortress, 1988.

Lapsley, Jacqueline. "Feeling Our Way: Love for God in Deuteronomy." *Catholic Biblical Quarterly* 65 (2003) 350–69.

Lehmann, Paul. *The Decalogue and a Human Future: The Meaning of the Commandments for Making and Keeping Human Life Human*. Grand Rapids: Eerdmans, 1995.

Kolb, Robert, and Timothy Wengert, editors. *The Book of Concord: The Confessions of the Evangelical Lutheran Church*. Minneapolis: Fortress, 2000.

Lewis, C. S. *Reflections on the Psalms*. New York: Harvest, 1964.

Long, Thomas G., and Leonora Tubbs Tisdale, editors. *Teaching Preaching as a Christian Practice: A New Approach to Homiletical Pedagogy*. Louisville: Westminster John Knox, 2008.

Mays, James L. "Jesus Came Preaching: A Study and Sermon on Mark 1:14–15." *Interpretation* 26 (1972) 30–41.

———. "Justice: Perspectives from the Prophets." *Interpretation* 37 (1983) 5–17.

———. *Psalms*. Interpretation. Louisville: Westminster John Knox, 1994.

McBride, S. Dean. "The Yoke of the Kingdom: An Exposition of Deuteronomy 6:4–5." *Interpretation* 27 (1973) 273–306.

Miller, Patrick D. "The Church's First Theologian." *Theology Today* 56 (1999) 293–96.

———. *Deuteronomy*. Interpretation. Louisville: Westminster John Knox, 1990.

———. *The God You Have: Politics and the First Commandment*. Facets. Minneapolis: Fortress, 2004.

———. "God's Other Stories: On the Margins of Deuteronomic Theology." In *Israelite Religion and Biblical Theology: Collected Essays*, 593–602. Journal for the Study of the Old Testament Supplement Series, 267. Sheffield: Sheffield Academic, 2000.

———. "In Praise and Thanksgiving." *Theology Today* 45 (1988) 180–88.

———. "January's Child." *Theology Today* 59 (2003) 525–28.

———. "A Strange Kind of Monotheism." *Theology Today* 54 (1997) 293–97.

———. "Studies in Hebrew Word Patterns." *Harvard Theological Review* 73 (1980) 79–89.

———. *The Ten Commandments*. Interpretation. Louisville: Westminster John Knox, 2009.

———. "A Theocentric Theologian of Hope: J. Christiaan Beker as Biblical Theologian." *The Princeton Seminary Bulletin* 16 (1995) 22–35.

———. *Theology Today: Reflections on the Bible and Contemporary Life*. Louisville: Westminster John Knox, 2006.

———. *They Cried to the Lord: The Form and Theology of Biblical Prayer*. Minneapolis: Fortress, 1994.

O'Connor, Kathleen M. *Jeremiah: Pain and Promise*. Minneapolis: Fortress, 2011.

Ouspensky, Leonid, and Vladimir Lossky. *The Meaning of Icons*. Rev. ed. Crestwood, NY: St. Vladimir's Seminary Press, 1999.

Presbyterian Church of the United States, General Assembly. *The Presbyterian Understanding and Use of Holy Scripture*. Louisville: Office of the General Assembly, 1992.

Prothero, Rowland E. *The Psalms in Human Life*. New York: Dutton, 1903.

Reumann, John. "Psalm 22 at the Cross: Lament and Thanksgiving for Jesus Christ." *Interpretation* 28 (1974) 39–58.

Rengstorf, Karl-Heinrich. "*hypēretēs*." In *Theological Dictionary of the New Testament*, edited by Gerhard Friedrich, translated and edited by Geoffrey W. Bromiley, 8:530–44. Grand Rapids: Eerdmans, 1972.

Sakenfeld, Katharine Doob. *Faithfulness in Action: Loyalty in Biblical Perspective*. Overtures to Biblical Theology. Philadelphia: Fortress, 1985.

Schweiker, William, and Michael Welker. "A New Paradigm of Theological and Biblical Inquiry." In *Power, Powerlessness, and the Divine: New Inquiries in Bible and Theology*, edited by Cynthia L. Rigby, 1–20. Scholars Press Studies in Theological Education. Atlanta: Scholars, 1997.

Seitz, Christopher R. "Old Testament or Hebrew Bible? Some Theological Considerations." *Pro Ecclesia* 5 (1996) 292–303.

———. "Old Testament or Hebrew Bible? Some Theological Considerations." In *Word without End: The Old Testament as Abiding Theological Witness*, 61–74. Grand Rapids: Eerdmans, 1997.

Shriver, Donald W., Jr. *An Ethic for Enemies: Forgiveness in Politics*. New York: Oxford University Press, 1995.

Soulen, R. Kendall. *The God of Israel and Christian Theology*. Minneapolis: Fortress, 1996.

Stark, Rodney. *For the Glory of God: How Monotheism Led to Reformations, Science, Witch-Hunts, and the End of Slavery*. Princeton: Princeton University Press, 2003.

Stevens, Marty. "On the Obedience of Trust: Recovering the Law as Gift." In *The Ten Commandments: The Reciprocity of Faithfulness*, edited by William P. Brown, 133–45. Library of Theological Ethics. Louisville: Westminster John Knox, 2004.

Taylor, Charles. *Sources of the Self: The Making of the Modern Identity*. Cambridge: Harvard University Press, 1989.

Tisdale, Leonora Tubbs. *Preaching as Local Theology and Folk Art*. Fortress Resources for Preaching. Minneapolis: Fortress, 1997.

———. *Prophetic Preaching: A Pastoral Approach*. Louisville: Westminster John Knox, 2010.

Weinberg, Stephen. *The First Three Minutes: A Modern View of the Origin of the Universe*. New York: Basic Books, 1977.

Westermann, Claus. *Elements of Old Testament Theology*. Translated by Douglas W. Stott. Atlanta: John Knox, 1982.

Scripture Index

Jeremiah

	33
1	93
1:5	76, 94
1:6	95
1:7	76, 95
1:8	96
1:17–19	96
7	50
7:3	78
23:16–22	88
32:17	33

Ezekiel

3:17	78

Daniel

3	60

Amos

7:10–17	75
7:15	76, 95
8:11–12	xi

Zechariah

8:4	147

~

New Testament

Matthew

	105, 127, 144
1:18–25	104
1:21	18
1:23	17
5	xii
5:21–26	39
6:24	59
22:23–33	71
25:31–40	149
25:35–36	117

Mark

	127, 144
1:22	89
1:27	89
13	99
13:32–39	99
14:1	101
15:1	101

Luke

	127, 144
1:46–55	108
1:51–53	109
2:1–20	108
2:8–20	104
4	83
4:16–21	22, 72
4:21–22	xii
9:1–6	91
9:51–62	65
16:13	59
19:41–44	144
19:45–48	89
20:1–8	88

John

13	128
13:1–20	127–31, 163–66
13:3	165
13:8	164
13:9–10	164
13:14	165
21:15–19	132–36

Acts

3:17–26	75
8:12	25
8:35	25
26:16	83

Lightning Source UK Ltd.
Milton Keynes UK
UKOW04f0428070917
308734UK00001B/180/P